Mrs. Orcutt's Driveway

By

C.V. Wooster

Published by TaciturnStudios.com – Taciturn Studios, Los Angeles, CA, USA

Disclaimer

This publication is intended to provide an accurate and well-researched portrayal of historical events and figures. While every effort has been made to ensure the facts are presented as faithfully as possible, historical interpretations can evolve over time, and new information may emerge that could further illuminate the subject matter. The events and characters depicted herein are based on the best available records, but certain elements of the narrative are interpretive, as is common in historical storytelling. For artistic purposes, some conversations and characters are composites, and while many characters are based on real individuals, certain dialogue and events have been fabricated for story continuity.

Any resemblance to actual persons, living or dead, other than public figures and those clearly identified in the text, is purely coincidental, unless otherwise noted as part of public record.

The author and publisher do not assume any responsibility for any inaccuracies or discrepancies that may arise. The stories shared in this book reflect the perspectives and understandings at the time of writing. Any opinions or conclusions expressed are those of the author and are not intended to serve as definitive judgments.

DEDICATION

For all the forgotten heroes—
The little guys, the lone women, the ones without
titles or headlines—
who stood their ground when it would've been
easier to step aside.

To those who write letters, plant flags, or simply say
"no"
when the world expects silence.

You may never be in the history books,
but you are the reason they matter.

—C. V. Wooster

ACKNOWLEDGEMENT

This set of Thank You's may seem as long as Mrs. Orcutt's Driveway, but rest assured that a story this old required many hands. This book could not have taken shape without the help of many generous organizations, departments, and individuals—some known, some anonymous, some who probably had no idea how much a comment, article, or archived image would spark something lasting.

To Lori — for your steady support and those well-timed nudges that kept me moving forward. Your patience and encouragement helped bring this story to life so others could discover a woman every bit as remarkable as you. I'm sure Margaret would agree.

Gratitude to those who offered interviews, insight, memories, photos, documents, and fragments, whether on or off the record: thank you. Your contributions gave form and texture to a story that had almost slipped through the cracks of history.

Special thanks to the vloggers who keep her story alive streaming on our screens, Route 66 preservationists, archivists, museum docents, desert historians, and Newberry Springs locals who recognized the quiet power of this tale and encouraged its telling. You reminded me that storytelling is a collective act, even when told through a single voice.

To those who sat for interviews, passed along old newspaper clippings, or small facts buried in dusty files—you may not be named here either, as most of you wished to preserve their anonymity, but your fingerprints are on every page.

This was never just about pavement and protest. It was about memory, place, and the strange beauty of a life etched into the land.

This became more than a project for me. It became a minor obsession, one I carried through rewrites, research holes, and midnight musings. I'm grateful to everyone who helped steer me through.

And finally—to Margaret "Bonnie" Orcutt: Thank you for standing your ground so that the rest of us might remember what it looks like when someone does. And to Kenneth Forest Orcutt, whose quiet partnership and enduring love added depth to every chapter of her life.

If this story moved you, I invite you to visit their virtual memorials, leave a digital flower or two, and carry a piece of their legacy forward. Because some lives—like some roads—are never meant to disappear.

They are now reunited in spirit, and, in a way, reunited online too:

Margaret's Memorial

https://www.findagrave.com/memorial/272205652/margaret_alberta-orcutt

Kenneth's Memorial

https://www.findagrave.com/memorial/73888697/kenneth-forest-orcutt

— C. V. Wooster

TABLE OF CONTENTS

PROLOGUE

The Mojave sun blazed over a solitary adobe house, its patched walls defying the desert's relentless heat. Inside, Margaret "Bonnie" Orcutt sat at a scarred oak table, her fingers hovering over her typewriter's black keys. The machine, her only weapon, gleamed faintly, ready to challenge the silence that threatened to erase her.

She drew a line in the sand with each letter she typed, a boundary against the surveyors' stakes that had pierced her land without consent.

The quiet in the room mirrored the wider, suffocating silence she faced. Months earlier, men with surveyor's stakes had come, driving their wooden markers into her land as if ownership were as simple as placing a claim. They hadn't asked. They hadn't explained.

They called it progress. Bonnie called it *theft*.

Her dirt path to Route 66—a fragile artery connecting her to the outside world—was no longer hers alone. Once her lifeline to the post office and the general store, it had become a racetrack for strangers, their reckless speed tearing through the desert as if it were nothing more than a backdrop to their arrogance.

Bonnie's jaw tightened as she glanced at the typewriter. Writing had become her ritual, a daily rebellion. Each letter was a declaration hurled into the void, even when the void answered with nothing.

Her gaze lingered on the pile of letters she'd already sent. Local officials had offered platitudes, their responses carefully crafted to say little. State agencies spoke of "the greater good" – a hollow term that cut deeper than any stake driven into her soil. The heat outside pressed against the walls, heavy as the weight of the silence that answered her fight.

And then, the clatter of the typewriter broke through. The rhythmic strikes of the keys filled the room. Each word carried the weight of her story, her anger, her determination. She wrote of the land's history, of the ancestors who had walked its sands before surveyors arrived with stakes and claims. She wrote of the desert's fragile ecosystem and the careless intrusion of speeding cars and thoughtless planners.

She paused for a moment, her hands still, and thought of the officials who might read this letter. Did they imagine her home at all? Could they picture the desert's endless horizons, or did they reduce her life to a case file—a name and address to be rubber-stamped and filed away?

The desert was unrelenting, indifferent to her struggle, but Bonnie drew strength from that. If the Mojave could endure, so could she.

Her breathing steadied as she pressed on, the words flowing until the page was full. She leaned back, her eyes scanning the letter. It was strong. It had to be.

The light outside softened, shifting to hues of amber and red as the day surrendered to dusk. Bonnie rose and moved to the window, her gaze tracing the endless horizon. The desert, ancient and resilient, didn't care about stakes or plans. It endured. Always.

As she sat by the window, gazing at the stretch of land soon to become the new interstate, she began to type: *'Dear President Lyndon B. Johnson...'*

CHAPTER 1

DUST AND PROMISES

Margaret "Bonnie" Orcutt knelt in her garden, coaxing life from the desert's stubborn soil. Her hands, rough from years of loss and labor, tended a creosote bush, its roots quiet defiance against the surveyors' stakes scarring her land. The Mojave's vast ridges stretched around her adobe home, whispering endurance, urging her to fight the highway threatening her sanctuary.

Long before settlers had arrived with axes and ambition, the Mojave Desert had not been empty. It had been alive, its soul intertwined with the Mojave people—kindred spirits to the land. To them, the desert had not been a challenge to be conquered but a companion to be understood. Its mountains had been sacred, its rivers lifelines, its sands a guardian that could nurture or judge. They had known its every secret: hidden springs that had quenched their thirst, healing herbs that had mended their wounds.

4

Together, they had thrived in harmony, their lives shaped by the rhythms of the desert. But change had arrived on boots and wagons, and with it had come intrusion.

The Mojave Desert, named after the resilient Mohave people, was a place where the land told stories of survival and transformation. It stretched across the southeastern corner of California, southwestern Nevada, and into parts of Arizona and Utah. Despite being the smallest and driest of North America's deserts, its history and ecology were anything but small.

The desert's landscape was shaped by a series of mountain ranges that rose sharply from the valleys, creating a dramatic play of light and shadow. The lowest point in North America, Death Valley, lay within its borders—an enduring reminder of the earth's constant upheaval. This dry, unforgiving land had witnessed centuries of change, yet life endured on its tough, cracked surface.

The iconic Joshua tree stood like a sentinel against the endless sky; its twisted branches etched into the horizon. The plants that called the Mojave home had evolved to withstand its extreme conditions. Creosote bushes, silver cholla cacti, and the vibrant Goldenhead flower all found ways to thrive in this harsh environment. Once, the desert had been dotted with mesquite forests, their deep roots tapping into hidden water sources, but many of these had been lost to the encroaching wave of settlement and industrialization.

The animals of the Mojave had learned to adapt. Bighorn sheep scaled its rocky slopes, while desert tortoises dug into its cool sands. Horned lizards and desert iguanas basked in the blistering heat, part of the delicate web of life that had persisted there for ages. Hidden springs and rare streams had provided refuge for creatures like the endangered Devils Hole pupfish, who clung to life in remnants of wetter times.

For thousands of years, the Mojave had been home to the Mohave people, who lived in deep connection with the land. They hunted, gathered, and respected the fragile balance of nature. Then, in the 18th century, Spanish explorers arrived. Francisco Garcés crossed the desert in 1776, documenting the people and their way of life. By the 19th century, American settlers and prospectors followed, carving their paths through the desert's shifting sands in search of gold, silver, and tungsten. The land yielded riches but paid a price, leaving scars that still marked the desert today.

In the 1850s, strangers set their sights on the Mojave, driven by ambitions as vast as the horizon. The United States government, eager to carve a path to California, deemed the desert expendable. Some called it progress. Others called it destiny. The Mojave people called it desecration.

They resisted fiercely. Their warriors stood against soldiers armed with rifles and cannons, wielding spears and bows shaped from the desert's mesquite trees. The Battle of Mojave roared across the sands, the air thick with smoke and cries. The Mojave fought not just for their land but for the spirit of the desert itself. Outmatched but unbroken, they left their mark on the valleys and mountains, their courage forever etched into the soul of the land. But the soldiers won, and the trail was built. More settlers followed, their wagons grinding deeper into the soil, each path pulling the desert further from its untouched beauty.

By the early 20th century, the scars of expansion had deepened. Paths became roads, and Route 66—dubbed the "Mother Road"—snaked through the Mojave's heart. To some, it was a promise of freedom and opportunity; to others, a harbinger of change. The settlers who arrived with its construction brought dreams of prosperity but also challenges the desert had never faced before.

The cycle of reshaping the Mojave began anew in the 1930s, as homesteaders arrived lured by the promise of cheap land and life-giving springs. To them, the Mojave was a blank canvas, a place where resilience and ambition could forge a new life. But the land they sought to tame had once been a thriving mesquite forest, stretching far beyond what is now the National Trails Highway.

The mesquite trees, gnarled and steadfast, were the desert's sentinels. Their deep roots tapped hidden reservoirs of water, sustaining life in a landscape that offered little freedom. They provided shade, nourishment, and fuel, embodying the resilience and balance of the Mojave. But even the mighty mesquite could not withstand the ambitions of men. Settlers felled the trees to fuel furnaces and support the mines of Calico, stripping the desert of its guardians. The loss was more than ecological—it was a wound to the desert's spirit, a reminder of the cost of progress.

Yet the Mojave endured. Its springs became lifelines for the settlers who stayed, and the cleared land offered new opportunities for those willing to adapt. Survival in the desert was a delicate balance, much like the mesquite's search for water. The settlers who thrived understood this balance, though the desert demanded their perseverance at every turn. As the decades passed, the Mojave bore witness to a relentless march of change. Expansion came with wooden stakes and steel markers, carving new paths through its vastness.

The Southern Emigrant Trail had been the first scar, followed by railroads and the Mother Road. These routes connected the desert to bustling cities, yet they also eroded its fragile isolation. During these changing times, World War II cast a long shadow over the country, and its effects rippled through the Mojave as well. As young men enlisted or were drafted, leaving their homes to fight across oceans, the war transformed the very fabric of American life. The landscape of the Mojave, too, was reshaped—military installations sprang up across its vast, empty spaces, and its harsh terrain became a proving ground for military training and testing. For the men and women who remained, rationing and blackouts were everyday concerns, but they also brought a sense of unity and shared purpose. Families in the small towns surrounding the desert struggled through wartime shortages, but the promise of peace brought hope for the future.

When the war ended, the Mojave, like the rest of the country, found itself at the crossroads of transformation. The post-war boom ignited a cultural shift—people who had once farmed or worked in the railroads now sought new lives in the growing cities. Suburbs expanded at a rapid pace, fueled by the optimism of returning soldiers and the promises of the GI Bill. The rise of the automobile and the interstate system further opened the Mojave to the demands of the modern world. The same desert that had been a symbol of isolation now became a bridge, a connection between the bustling metropolises of California and the distant promise of the American

Dream. Yet, with every new highway and home, the Mojave's identity was slowly being erased, swallowed by the demands of a nation eager to forget the silence of the desert and the lives that had once thrived in its quiet shadows.

In this background, the struggles of Margaret "Bonnie" Orcutt began to unfold. The stakes driven into her land were not just markers for a road; they were symbols of disregard, of a system that saw her home as an obstacle rather than a sanctuary. Like the desert itself, Bonnie had learned to endure. The government's plans seemed inevitable, but inevitability did not mean rightness.

From her small adobe home, Bonnie fought back—not with weapons but with her typewriter. Her letters, written in the dim glow of her living room, were not pleas for help but declarations of defiance. Her words carried the weight of the Mojave's spirit, a fight for preservation against the relentless tide of bureaucracy.

The Mojave had shaped her resolve, and its harshness mirrored in her tenacity. Like the mesquite that once stood strong, Bonnie dug deep, seeking strength in the roots of her connection to the land. Her struggle was not just personal but universal—a continuation of the timeless battle between preservation and progress. The echoes of the Mojave people's resistance resounded in her fight. A century earlier, the Mojave warriors had stood against rifles and cannons, their bravery etched into the soul of the desert. Now, the desert bore witness again. Margaret "Bonnie" Orcutt, armed only with her typewriter and her unshakable determination, prepared to carry that legacy forward. Her battle for autonomy and survival was not new—it was a fight as eternal and unyielding as the Mojave itself.

CHAPTER 2

THE HARPIST OF RICHMOND

Margaret Alberta "Bonnie" McMains was born on September 7, 1909, in Boone County, Indiana, where the rolling farmland stretched wide, and communities thrived on connection and hard work. She was the only and eldest daughter of Wolford E. McMains and Fern Caroline Meyer McMains.

From three years until she was eighteen, Bonnie grew up in Indianapolis, where her father owned a Chevrolet dealership. In 1927, they moved to Richmond, Indiana—a town humming with the promise of early 20th-century progress. Her father's Buick dealership stood as a symbol of the burgeoning automobile age, a monument to innovation and opportunity that would subtly shape her perspective on life.

Bonnie's childhood was alive with the energy of a bustling household, one of five children in a home where tradition and ambition coexisted. Amid the clamor of siblings and the steady hum of her father's business, Bonnie's innate curiosity began to take root. She displayed a keen intellect and an artistic flair, both of which would become defining characteristics of her life. Anchored by the values of diligence, faith, and an appreciation for history, her formative years instilled a sense of purpose and resilience.

Faith played a quiet but pivotal role in Bonnie's life. She was said by many to follow Christian Science, a religious movement founded in the 19th century by Mary Baker Eddy. Eddy, a writer and teacher, emphasized the power of spiritual and mental healing, believing that faith and thought could influence physical well-being. Rooted like an old mesquite, her faith aligned with her independent nature and visionary outlook, reinforcing her faith in resilience, self-reliance, and the boundless potential of the mind.

Bonnie's intellectual pursuits mirrored the breadth of her talents. A graduate of Earlham College, Butler University, DePauw University, and the Arthur Jordan Conservatory of Music, she majored in biochemistry with a focus on plant biology. Her research on black walnut trees garnered recognition in scientific circles, yet her scholarly endeavors were only part of her identity. She was also an accomplished concert-level harpist, her performances evoking the same grace and precision she applied to her academic work.

During World War II, Bonnie, trained by her father to be a crack shot in her Indiana youth, shifted her focus to production roles that bolstered the military effort while also leveraging her sharpshooting expertise to teach pistol marksmanship to over a hundred new police officers, thus helping replace those who had gone to war. With the war effort demanding the contributions of every available man and woman, Bonnie stepped up, putting her skills to work in support of the cause.

She also worked at Hayes Track Appliance Company before joining her father's business, demonstrating a pragmatic approach to problem-solving that complemented her artistic sensibilities. These experiences honed her ability to adapt and endure—qualities that would serve her well in the years to come.

By 1943, Bonnie was a cornerstone of Richmond's cultural scene. Her leadership in the Richmond Civic Theater reflected her devotion to preserving history and fostering artistic excellence. An article featured in Palladium-Item lauded her meticulous work in curating a collection of period costumes for a production of *Ah, Wilderness!* The garments, crafted with care and steeped in local history, brought authenticity to the stage, a testament to Bonnie's reverence for the past and her eye for detail.

Her artistic talents extended beyond the stage. Bonnie was a skilled musician, mastering multiple instruments and performing with orchestras in New York. Her interpretations of Bach and Chopin earned her accolades for their emotional depth and technical brilliance. These musical achievements connected her to a broader artistic community, deepening her appreciation for the transformative power of culture and creativity.

In 1948, Bonnie's life shifted with love's sudden spark. At a community event, under the glow of lanterns, she sat at her harp, her fingers dancing delicately across the strings, coaxing a melody so ethereal it hushed the crowd. The piece—a tender lament—carried a quiet longing, each plucked note weaving a bittersweet tale that stirred the heart. Kenneth Orcutt, standing at the room's edge, was transfixed. Her music, her grace, her fleeting smile as she played—it was as if she'd reached into his soul.

It wasn't just the music, though it was exquisite—it was her. The way her head tilted slightly as she played, the quiet smile that flickered when she glanced at the audience, and the graceful way she carried herself, as though she belonged in a world far more refined than the small hall they occupied.

When she finished the waltz, the applause was thunderous, but he hardly noticed. All he could think of was the way her music seemed to reach out to him, as if she had unknowingly shared a part of her soul. It was at that moment he decided he needed to speak to her—not just about the music, but about the person who could create something so achingly beautiful. But Bonnie felt his gaze, a warmth that quickened her pulse. When they spoke after, his words were earnest, his eyes alight with admiration.

Kenneth, son of Mrs. H. E. Hagaman of Inglewood, California, was a nationally recognized diver selected for the canceled 1940 Helsinki Olympics. He was dashing and confident, with a magnetic personality that drew people in. She, in turn, was deeply taken by his looks, his adventurous spirit, and his natural charisma.

Their courtship had been brief but filled with tender moments. They strolled through quiet town streets, sharing dreams of the future, and spent evenings where she played piano and harp, and he listened in awe of her talent. Kenneth often spoke of the life they could build together, painting vivid pictures of adventure and possibilities.

An alumnus of Iowa State College and Compton College, Kenneth was also a chinchilla broker and had served as a personnel supervisor for a Los Angeles transit corporation. His mother, a renowned chinchilla rancher, held grand champion stock in the U.S., which further impressed her with the intriguing world he was connected to.

By the time they stood together on their wedding day in 1948, Bonnie was ready to leave her small-town Indiana roots behind, confident that their shared dreams and his promises of adventure would lead her to a remarkable future out west. They were united in marriage in a beautiful ceremony at the home of the bride's parents. A man named Dr. H. T. Reinecke officiated the double-ring ceremony, witnessed by the immediate families of the couple.

The living room had been transformed into an enchanting setting, with four seven-branch candelabras adorned with ferns standing before the fireplace. The room featured Snow-White roses, white snapdragons, and a stunning vase of red roses on the piano. Accounts from the local papers like Palladium-Item stated that Mrs. Marjorie Beck Lohman provided sacred music at the piano, accompanied by a quartet consisting of Mrs. William Shoemaker, Miss Alice Ellen Page, Richard Little, and Elmer Varnell. The musical program included selections such as Andante by Mrs. Lohman, Holy,

Holy, Holy by the quartet, and Adoration by Borowski, played as the bride walked to the altar.

The bride, Ms Bonnie, looked radiant in an eighteenth-century-inspired gown of sunglow ivory satin-backed crepe. The gown featured a tightly fitted bodice with lace-down detail, an ivory tulle yoke creating a drop-shoulder effect, and three-quarter-length sleeves trimmed with pleated silk lace and delicate bows. The heavily gathered flowing skirt revealed a double row of lace ruffles and an appliquéd rose of pearls. The ensemble was completed with a chinchilla fur band along the hemline, and a matching chinchilla stole cape gifted by the groom.

The bride's hair was adorned with heirloom ivory silk lace and a pearl tiara. She carried a family heirloom handkerchief and Psalm book decorated with silk roses, satin ribbons, and a single white orchid. Her ivory satin slippers featured pearl accents.

The matron of honor, Mrs. Wren McMains, wore a pearl-gray silk taffeta gown with a tunic and long fitted sleeves, accented by a corsage of white roses and violet sweet peas. The bride's mother wore a powdered rose-pink crepe dress with a pink globelia corsage, while the groom's mother chose a Halcyon blue crepe dress paired with a corsage of salmon-colored sweet peas and white roses.

A buffet supper followed the ceremony, featuring a three-tier cake encircled with white gardenias and sweet peas.

The scene exuded sophistication and grace, a reflection of the bride's life at that moment—a life of refinement and promise.

Following their wedding, the couple honeymooned through the Ozarks, Catalina Island, and Big Bear Lake. It marked the beginning of what Bonnie envisioned as a life of shared dreams and mutual triumphs.

CHAPTER 3

ROOTS AND WINGS: BONNIE'S GROUND, KENNETH'S SKY

Bonnie Orcutt was a woman of quiet convictions and steady hands. She carried herself with the grace of someone who had long ago learned that life was best handled with patience, a sharp wit, and a sense of humor that could soften the hardest days. Beneath the weathered beams of their house that they had built together, she put her stake in the soil with daily rituals that tethered their union to something deeper than routine.

Every morning, she would rise before the sun, the soft creak of the floorboards beneath her feet echoing through the stillness of the house. Kenneth's snoring would carry from the bedroom as she stoked the fire in the kitchen stove, her fingers deft and sure. By the time he stirred, she'd have a pot of coffee brewing, its earthy aroma filling the air. She'd tease him, her lips quirking as she poured his cup. "Some days, Kenneth Orcutt, I think the only reason you married me was for this coffee."

Kenneth would grin, his face weathered but still ruggedly handsome. "Not true, Bonnie. There's the pie, too."

Their mornings together were often spent in companionable silence. Kenneth would read the paper while Bonnie tended to the garden just outside the kitchen window. The garden was hers alone, a patch of land that seemed to mirror her own resilience. Rows of marigolds and lavender swayed gently in the breeze, the herbs she grew finding their way into nearly every meal.

But life in the Orcutt household wasn't all serenity. Kenneth, with his relentless drive and boundless curiosity, had a way of inviting chaos. Bonnie often found herself at the center of his grand ideas. There was a time when he decided to set up a solar panel system in their backyard, convinced it would reduce their electricity bills. Bonnie watched him tinker with wires, brackets, and instruction manuals for three days, her arms crossed and an amused smirk on her lips, until the panels finally powered a single lightbulb. "A whole light," she teased, clapping slowly. "We're practically off the grid."

When it promptly toppled over in the next storm, she merely said, "At least the chickens enjoyed the show."

Their arguments were as passionate as their love. Bonnie had a fiery streak, and Kenneth, stubborn as a mule, often clashed with her when his ambitions grew too wild. One particularly heated disagreement involved his purchase of a dilapidated truck he swore he could fix. "Kenneth, that thing's more rust than metal," Bonnie had said, her hands on her hips. "It'll be a miracle if it doesn't fall apart the moment you touch it."

He grinned, undeterred. "Miracles happen, don't they?"

And yet, for all their differences, they moved as a pair, each one anchoring the other. Bonnie, with her pragmatism, balanced Kenneth's restless ingenuity.

Kenneth's frequent business trips, however, began to carve gaps in their shared rhythm. He'd sweep into town after weeks away, his suitcase brimming with new plans for the chinchilla farm, only to leave again for another city, another speech. One evening, after a long absence, he burst through the door, his voice booming with excitement. "Bonnie, the San Diego investors are in! We're expanding!" She smiled, her heart lifting at his energy, but as she set a plate of cornbread before him, a quiet ache settled in her chest. His visits were fleeting, each departure leaving the house too still. "You're always chasing the next big thing," she said softly, her fingers tracing the table's grain. "Sometimes I wish you'd stay long enough to see what we've already built." Kenneth pulled her close, his laughter warm, but her smile hid a longing for the days when their mornings together were unbroken.

Bonnie often stood alone in their garden during his absences, the morning silence mirroring her thoughts. She missed his laughter, his wild ideas, even his stubbornness, but she also felt the weight of managing their home alone. One afternoon, as she pruned lavender, a neighbor stopped by, noticing her distant gaze. "Kenneth off again?" he asked. Bonnie nodded, forcing a smile. "Busy man, my husband. But I keep the place running." Her voice held pride, but her heart carried a flicker of resentment.

As a man of many talents, Kenneth F. Orcutt was known across Southern California as a pioneer in the burgeoning chinchilla industry. He possessed a charisma that could transform a modest endeavor into a grand vision. His story was one of passion and persistence, marked by his unique ability to blend business acumen with infectious optimism.

In the late 1940s, he emerged as a prominent figure in the chinchilla industry, an enterprise that captivated his imagination and fueled his entrepreneurial spirit. Speaking to the Riverside Optimist Club, he shared his dreams for the future of chinchilla farming. "There are currently 200,000 chinchillas in the United States," he proclaimed, "but we are aiming for 7 million to establish a robust fur industry." His enthusiasm was palpable, and his words inspired many to see these small, silky-furred creatures as the cornerstone of a lucrative future.

Kenneth's passion for chinchillas wasn't just professional—it was deeply personal. He often spoke at local organizations, blending humor and expertise to captivate his audience. At a Kiwanis Club luncheon, he introduced two live chinchillas as "guests of honor," charming the crowd with anecdotes about their habits and care. His playful speech, titled "Love Nest Wanted," was a perfect recipe for whimsy and wit, making him a sought-after speaker in civic circles.

Finally, in February 1951, he opened an ambitious retail chinchilla farm on Sepulveda Boulevard in Manhattan Beach. The "Brown Adobe" property, transformed into a tropical paradise, became a landmark in the South Bay. The farm boasted an elaborate Chinese-Hawaiian theme, with lush tropical plants, bamboo and rattan furniture, and chandeliers adorned with orchids. Kenneth and his wife, Bonnie, welcomed visitors with warmth and professionalism, showcasing their shared dedication to the business.

Bonnie, a partner in every sense, brought her own flair to the venture. Her exceptional sense of music and her natural grace complemented Kenneth's dynamic personality. Together, they created an environment that was as much about education and experience as it was about sales. Visitors to the farm were treated not just to the sight of chinchillas but to an experience that left them enchanted by the Orcutts' vision.

Kenneth's ventures extended beyond the United States. He played a pivotal role in introducing chinchilla farming to Japan, shipping pairs of prized animals overseas under carefully monitored conditions. This endeavor not only opened a new market but also demonstrated his knack for innovation and expansion. "The chinchilla enjoys 400 years of history and is incredibly valuable," he often said, educating audiences about the animal's origins and its potential in the global market.

His unwavering optimism was a cornerstone of his success. Whether addressing a local club or planning his next big move, he exuded a confidence that inspired those around him. He believed in the promise of the chinchilla industry and in the broader idea that small, deliberate steps could lead to monumental change.

Together, the couple shared many loving evenings. Bonnie would linger by the window of their home, a shadow, as Kenneth would tinker with yet another contraption—a prototype for an innovative chinchilla habitat he insisted would revolutionize the industry.

One particular evening, as the sun dipped below the horizon, his laughter echoed through the twilight as he held up a piece of wood to the fading light, oblivious to the darkening clouds gathering on the horizon. Bonnie sat at the kitchen table, a notebook open before her, scribbling a list of dreams she'd been harboring for years. "Build a home for unwed mothers," she wrote in neat cursive. "Create a sanctuary in the desert." Each item carried a piece of her heart, a future she longed to share with Kenneth. Yet, as she glanced out the window at his shadowed figure, a pang of doubt crept in. Would there be enough time for all of it?

Later that night, as they lay in bed, Kenneth spoke of future plans with his characteristic zeal—expanding their farm, taking the business international, and even the idea of a cross-country speaking tour. His voice brimmed with energy as he shifted to another passion: the sky. Among his many loves, flying held a special place in his heart. Long before chinchillas had consumed his entrepreneurial dreams, Kenneth had found solace in the freedom of flying aircraft as a licensed pilot. "You know," he said, his voice softening, "sometimes I think if I could live my life up there, just above the clouds, I would. There's nothing like it, Bonnie. The world feels endless, full of possibilities."

Bonnie listened, her chest shrinking with both pride and unease. Kenneth's love for flying had always made her nervous, though she'd never voiced it. His bold confidence, a strength in his business endeavors, sometimes felt less suited to the cockpit, where caution was key. Those closest to him, sensing the risks in his fearless approach, often hesitated to join him in the air.

As Bonnie thought of her folded list in the bedside drawer, her secret hope for a quieter, more purposeful life together. "You dream so big, Kenneth," she whispered, her voice barely audible over the wind that had begun to howl outside. "But I wonder, do we ever stop to ask what we might lose in chasing those dreams?" Kenneth chuckled and reached for her hand, his grip warm and reassuring, but in the dark, neither could see the worry etched across the other's face.

CHAPTER 4

WHEN THE SKY FELL TWICE

In the months following Kenneth and Bonnie's decision to open the farm to visitors, life had settled into a harmonious rhythm.

The days were full, but not overwhelming, marked by the steady hum of work and the laughter they shared in the quiet moments. Visitors came from far and wide to see the farm and hear Kenneth's charismatic presentations.

Her will was carved into the rock of their shared vision, as she watched Kenneth captivate guests with his stories, a soft smile tugging at her lips as her husband enthralled the guests with his stories. Together, they were building something special, something enduring.

But as much as Kenneth was at home on their farm, he was also a man of the world. His ambitions often called him away, whisking him off to conferences, exhibitions, and meetings with other pioneers in the industry. Bonnie had grown accustomed to the ebb and flow of his absences.

One crisp autumn morning, the golden light filtering through the kitchen window cast a warm glow over the wooden table as Kenneth burst into the room, his voice brimming with infectious excitement. He slid into his chair, clutching a fork like a conductor's baton, and waved it animatedly over his half-eaten plate of eggs. "Bonnie, you won't believe this—I've been invited to showcase our chinchillas at a massive exhibition in Detroit!" he exclaimed, his eyes sparkling with ambition. "It's a golden chance to strut our farm across the Midwest, shake hands with top breeders, and maybe even land some big deals. This could be huge for us—really put us on the map!" He leaned closer, his fork punctuating each word with a flourish, his enthusiasm filling the room like a melody.

Bonnie set her coffee cup down with a soft clink, the steam curling upward as she met his gaze with a smile that radiated pride yet carried a faint shadow of unease. "Oh, Kenneth, that does sound wonderful," she said, her voice warm but tinged with a quiet hesitation. "I'm so proud of you—your passion for this is something else. But I'll miss you terribly while you're gone. The house feels like a cavern every time you leave, echoing with your absence." Her fingers tightened around the cup, the porcelain cool against her skin, betraying the worry she fought to conceal as her heart gave a small, anxious flutter.

Kenneth's grin stretched wider, a boyish delight dancing in his eyes as he leaned across the table, his chair creaking under his eagerness. "I'll be back before you can blink, Bonnie—faster than you can miss me! And this time, I'm taking the reins myself. Got the plane all prepped and gleaming—just me, the open sky, and a straight shot to Detroit. Imagine it!" His voice soared with the thrill of the adventure, his hands sketching invisible flight paths in the air.

Bonnie's breath hitched, a sharp intake that stilled the room for a moment, her eyes flickering with a mix of concern and unspoken fear. "Oh, Kenneth," she murmured, her voice firm yet threaded with a tremor she couldn't quite suppress, "you be careful up there. Promise me you'll watch every cloud and every gust—those skies can be treacherous." Her hands clasped the cup tighter, as if anchoring herself against the dread creeping into her chest.

"Always, my love—always," Kenneth reassured her, his tone softening as he rose slightly, leaning over to press a tender kiss to her forehead. His lips lingered there, warm and grounding, a silent vow against the wildness of his dreams, while Bonnie closed her eyes, clinging to the fleeting comfort of his touch amid the storm of worry brewing within her.

The morning of his departure arrived far too quickly. Bonnie busied herself preparing his things—packing a small lunch, ironing his favorite shirt, and double-checking his itinerary. The house felt different without him, quieter but heavier, as though it anticipated what was to come.

That night, Bonnie sat by the window with a book, though she found it impossible to focus on the words. The wind had picked up, rustling the trees outside and sending shadows dancing across the walls. She glanced at the clock on the mantel, willing time to move faster, and pressed her hand to her chest. Her heart felt unusually heavy, beating harder than it should. "It's nothing," she told herself. "Just nerves."

The next morning, Bonnie moved through her chores with a knot in her stomach that refused to loosen, each task— sweeping the porch, tending her lavender—feeling heavier under the weight of her thoughts. *Where was Kenneth now?* Perhaps charming a room full of investors, his voice bright with the promise of their chinchilla empire, or maybe he was in a dusty airfield, gazing at the sky with that reckless gleam in his eyes. She ached for his call, for the soothing cadence of his voice to fill the quiet house, to hear his excitement spill over, painting dreams she both loved and feared.

By mid-afternoon, Bonnie went about her day, her hands steady as she folded a dish towel, her heart lifted by thoughts of Kenneth's flight. She pictured his warm laughter and the stories of the skies he'd share, a quiet joy blooming at the life they were weaving together. The farm, their dreams, his boundless enthusiasm for flying—all felt vibrant, full of promise. She hummed softly, expecting his call any moment to inform her that he had landed safely.

It was just before dusk when the knock came at the door. Bonnie froze, the sound reverberating through the silent house. She wiped her hands on her apron and approached the door slowly. Suddenly, a strange weight pressed down on her chest.

The man standing on the porch was unfamiliar, dressed in a dark suit with a hat clutched tightly in his hands. His face was solemn, his eyes filled with a quiet sadness that spoke before his words did.

"Mrs. Orcutt?" he asked gently.

Bonnie nodded, her throat suddenly dry.

"I'm sorry to have to tell you this," the man began, his voice low and steady. "There's been an accident."

The rest of his words blurred into an indistinct hum. Bonnie swayed where she stood, gripping the doorframe for support. Her knees buckled, but she remained upright, held there by sheer will. "And?" she whispered. The man's voice grew softer, almost apologetic. "The plane went down near Burlington, Iowa. There were no survivors." He had been piloting the aircraft himself, no doubt with the same determined spirit that had guided so many of his ventures. But even the most steadfast of souls cannot escape the unpredictability of the skies.

Two days later, the details of the crash surfaced, painting a sobering picture of the final moments. Kenneth was guiding the plane through turbulent skies when a sudden downdraft wrestled the aircraft into a fatal descent. Alongside Kenneth, aged forty, were two passengers: L. B. Sandy of Long Beach, California, and Irene Doris Cobell of Youngstown, Ohio. The trio had been on a flight from Kirksville, Missouri, bound for Detroit, Michigan.

Fate, however, played a cruel hand. Richard McCormick of Manhattan Beach, who had initially planned to join the flight, decided at the last minute to drive to Detroit instead, citing overcrowding in the small plane. "It was a matter of space," he later shared, his voice heavy with the weight of what might have been.

Kenneth's love for flying had been a defining part of his life, a passion he spoke of with awe and reverence. "Sometimes I think if I could live my life up there, just above the clouds, I would," he had once told Bonnie. Those words, spoken in the intimacy of their shared evenings, now carried a bittersweet resonance.

In the days that followed, Bonnie moved as though in a dream, her world muted and gray. She went through the motions of planning Kenneth's funeral, but the reality of his absence felt impossible to grasp. On the morning of the service, she stood in front of the mirror, her hands trembling as she fastened a black ribbon to her modest dress. Her reflection was unfamiliar, her face pale and drawn, her eyes hollow from sleepless nights.

Funeral services for Kenneth were held at Doan & Son Mortuary, with Dr. Anthony Meengs presiding over the ceremony. The burial was followed at Earlham Cemetery, a quiet place befitting a man who sought so much yet always seemed grounded by the people he loved. In accordance with the family's wishes, the casket remained closed.

Bonnie sat in the front row, her hands clasped tightly in her lap. She listened as Dr. Meengs spoke of Kenneth's boundless energy, his vision, and the lives he had touched.

In the hours after the service, the community enveloped Bonnie in a wave of support. Neighbors from nearby houses arrived with casseroles and wildflower bouquets, their faces etched with sympathy as they shared stories of Kenneth's infectious laughter and grand dreams. The women of the local church auxiliary gathered in her kitchen, brewing coffee and murmuring words of comfort, while men from the chinchilla farm offered to tend her garden and livestock. Their kindness warmed the cold edges of her grief, yet each condolence reminded her of the void Kenneth had left, a presence no one could replace.

But as days turned to weeks, the visitors dwindled. The neighbors' calls grew sparse, their lives reclaiming their rhythms. Her parents had grown frail with age, and Bonnie shielded them from the depths of her grief, unwilling to burden their weary hearts. In their presence, she wore a mask of healing, her smiles forced but convincing, her voice quiet as she spoke of tending the garden or farm chores, all to grant them peace. But when they eventually returned to their home in Indiana, leaving her in the quiet house, Bonnie's facade crumbled. Alone, she wandered rooms still echoing with Kenneth's laughter, haunted by the dreams they'd woven together—dreams now as distant as the desert stars.

One day, Bonnie lingered by the grave long after sunset. The autumn air was cool, and the sky above was streaked with pink and gold. She knelt beside the mound of earth, her fingers tracing the edges of the headstone. "You dreamed so big, Kenneth," she whispered, her voice breaking. "And you left so much behind."

As the weeks turned into months, Bonnie tried to find her footing in a world that felt foreign without Kenneth. The farm became her refuge; the routines she once shared with him were now a lifeline to the life they had built together.

One evening, as she sat alone by the window, her notebook in her lap, she opened to the list she had written months earlier. The words stared back at her, fragile but unwavering: "Build a home for unwed mothers. Create a sanctuary in the desert." She picked up her pen and added a new line beneath them: "Carry on his dream."

The wind stirred outside, rattling the panes, but Bonnie remained still. She would grieve for Kenneth every day, she knew, but she would also honor him— in the life they had shared and in the dreams he had left behind.

As Bonnie and her family reeled from Kenneth's sudden passing, tragedy struck again. Just six weeks later, her father, W. E. McMains, succumbed to an illness while revisiting his daughter in California. W. E. McMains, once a prominent businessman in Richmond, had built a life of enterprise and integrity, running Chevrolet and Buick dealerships before turning his focus to the Stolle Packing Company on Liberty Avenue during World War II.

In 1953, her father, alongside his wife, had traveled to Manhattan Beach to check up on Bonnie, only for fate to deal yet another cruel blow. The visit was meant to mend, to wrap her in the quiet strength of family, but fate, unrelenting, struck another devastating blow. On a hushed Sunday night, he slipped away, leaving an ache that echoed through those he loved. Four officers she had trained during World War II drove the police escort cars at her father's funeral. His legacy—of tireless work, unwavering devotion, and a love that anchored his family—lived on in the hearts of his wife, daughter, and son, W. E. McMains.

CHAPTER 5

A WORLD OF HER OWN

In the span of six weeks, Bonnie lost the two men who had shaped her world—first her beloved husband and now her cherished father. The weight of it pressed on her, suffocating and inescapable. The days blurred into one another, filled with the hollow rituals of mourning and sorrow. Mornings began with the deafening silence of an empty home; evenings ended with the flicker of candlelight against walls that had once echoed with laughter.

At first, she clung to routine, believing that work would steady her, but the place felt different now—diminished, as if it had lost its heart. Letters of condolence arrived in careful, sympathetic script, yet none could fill the void. Friends and family encouraged her to take time to heal, but time only made the absence more profound.

Then came the lawsuit.

In April 1954, just when Bonnie thought she had endured the worst, she found herself in the crosshairs of the legal system. A Long Beach woman, Mrs. Lucille Sandy, filed a $50,000 lawsuit against her, seeking damages for the death of her husband, Lacy B. Sandy. He had been aboard Kenneth's ill-fated flight to Michigan, and now, Bonnie was being accused of negligence by association. The suit alleged that Kenneth, holding only a student pilot's license, should never have carried passengers, implying that his inexperience had led to the tragedy.

The case made her grief worse, forcing her to relive the loss under the harsh scrutiny of the public eye. She attended hearings, her hands clasped tightly in her lap, listening as lawyers dissected the final moments of her husband's life. The legal jargon, the cold and impersonal discussion of his death, felt like another kind of theft—stripping away what little she had left of him. And yet, beneath the sorrow, other emotions simmered.

Was she angry at Kenneth? Furious that his actions—his recklessness, perhaps—had not only taken him from her but had dragged her into this legal nightmare? At times, she wondered if the courtroom whispers carried judgment, if people saw her not as a grieving widow but as someone complicit in the accident. The weight of it pressed on her, compounded by a gnawing fear: Would she be held financially responsible? Would she lose what little stability she had left?

Then, in September 1954, the attack happened. As reported by The Daily Breeze, California, someone had slashed the leather cover of her parked car, unfastening it and leaving the damage exposed like an open wound. There was no clear message, no note, just a silent warning of vandalism. Was it random? A cruel prank? Or had someone decided she needed to be punished further?

It was the final confirmation of what she had begun to suspect—she was not just grieving; she was being watched, judged, perhaps even hated. The city she had once called home now felt hostile, its streets filled with unseen threats. She found herself glancing over her shoulder more often, locking doors she had never thought twice about before. The attack wasn't just an act of vandalism; it was a violation, an intrusion into what little peace she had left. Manhattan Beach held too many ghosts, too many accusations, too many shadows stretching toward her like grasping hands. She could not stay. Staying meant living under the weight of suspicion in a place where even inanimate objects—her home, her car, the very air she breathed—seemed to whisper that she no longer belonged.

By the time the lawsuit was resolved, Bonnie had made up her mind. She had to leave. She needed to start over. But where does a woman go when she is untethered from the life she once knew?

The answer didn't come from memory or sentimentality—it came from the earth itself. Bonnie chose Newberry not for its desolation but for a spark of possibility that flickered in its vast, sun-scorched expanse. After Kenneth's death, she sought a place where she could root herself anew, where the Mojave's rugged silence could hold her grief and fuel her purpose. Newberry's barren beauty called to her—a canvas of solitude where she could build something tangible, something hers, born from the land's raw potential and her own unyielding resolve.

The land, rich in specific mineral properties—sand with just the right texture, maybe even trace amounts of bitumen— was ideal for the model kits she dreamed of producing. She envisioned packets of this native clay tucked alongside tiny architectural pieces, ready for hobbyists to build miniature homes or scenes. It was a niche vision, perhaps even ahead of its time, but entirely hers. She hadn't needed to ship in material; she could dig it from her own backyard. This wasn't nostalgia—it was strategy. A practical, hands-in-the-dirt pursuit of a dream born not from memory but from resourcefulness.

Still, there was something poetic about it. The beach and the desert—both built on sand, but one with an excess of water, the other defined by its

41

absence. She had spent years by the shore, letting the tide pull at her ankles, the saltwater filling her lungs. Now, she would go where the waves could never reach, where the land stretched out dry and unyielding, offering no illusions of comfort. The ocean had always returned what it took—a shell, a fragment of driftwood, a piece of glass polished smooth by time. The desert, she suspected, would not be so kind.

Perhaps that was exactly what she needed—a place that demanded nothing in return. A refuge where she could lose herself in solitude, where her grief would not echo through courtroom walls or be reduced to a monetary figure. A place where no one would come searching for her. This sanctuary of isolation was meant to be her new beginning.

Arriving in the Mojave in mid-1950s, Bonnie's vision was as vast as the desert itself. She found an ideal location for her new home in a 100-acre parcel just east of Newberry, where the land stretched in a sun-scorched tapestry of sand and sagebrush, unbroken but for the distant silhouette of the Calico Mountains. It was here, in this rugged expanse kissed by relentless sun and whispering winds, that Bonnie would begin her journey of carving out a life, her determination as unyielding as the earth she claimed.

She found the land through a realtor—Robert and Ruth Shears of Shears Realty. A house was out of the question—at least for now. The desert was not kind to those who built carelessly, and Bonnie was determined to do things right. A temporary solution was needed, something small, something she could manage alone. The idea of a travel trailer emerged not as a grand plan but as a practical necessity. It wasn't luxury, but it was shelter, a place to sleep while she figured out how to transform this barren expanse into a home.

At the heart of her desert domain sat her Airstream trailer, polished silver and stoic, a gleaming capsule of solitude and survival. It was her first true shelter in the Mojave, parked beneath the vast sky like a moon landed among creosote and sage.

Nearby stood two corrugated metal sheds, utilitarian but essential—they housed what she called her "Littlest Lumberyard," the humble beginnings of a model kit company she dreamed would one day put her desert clay into hobby shops across the country. Inside, stacked alongside tools and bags of hand-sifted earth, were three or four antique cars— though "antique" only in the sense that time had passed since she first drove them. One of the most clearly remembered by one of her distant relatives was a 1948 Buick, solid and stylish, a car that seemed made for long desert roads and determined women. She kept them all in running order, each vehicle a symbol of a life lived in motion, even in a place that stood still.

On the other hand, the small travel trailer was in stark contrast to the home she had once shared with Kenneth. The trailer, a modest aluminum shell with narrow windows and compact living space, housed a small bed, a fold-down table, and a small propane stove. It had been built for the road, for a life of movement and possibility.

Perhaps that's why Bonnie had anchored it within her home. It was practical, yes—a ready-made shelter as she worked to shape the adobe walls around it—but there was something more. A part of her, however small, must have liked the idea of keeping one foot in both worlds: the illusion of being a stylish vagabond, free to take to the road at a moment's notice, even as she built a home meant to last.

She had decorated the trailer as if it were a tiny second home, a cozy retreat tucked inside the larger space she was crafting. Maybe, on some nights, she even found comfort in its wooden-walled interior, the kind of spellbinding quiet that made a place feel safe—when the desert air was still, and the world felt far away. It was both a contradiction and a compromise, an acknowledgment that even as she laid down roots in the Mojave, a part of her still carried the dream of movement, of open highways and unburdened escape.

But she had no intention of staying within those walls forever. Slowly, painstakingly, she began constructing an adobe house around the trailer itself. The trailer became her bedroom, nestled within the growing structure, while the rest of the house took shape around it.

Mrs. Margaret Orcutt's home was a puzzle of ingenuity, its quirks as striking as the woman herself. What initially appeared to be a garage door at the east end, likely for hauling a trailer in or out, hid a shower and storage nook instead. The trailer, swallowed whole by the house, was woven into its very bones.

Since the very beginning, she longed to create something truly transformative—something that could serve others. With the help of an early Newberry homesteader, William H. Smith, she carved out a quarter-mile-long reservoir on her property, its waters shimmering under the relentless desert sun. A marvel of engineering and sheer willpower, it became more than just a body of water—it felt alive, almost sentient. Stranger still was the living room—Bonnie might've called it the lake room—nestled between the trailer and the water, with only a narrow hallway to pass food through to the kitchen, skirting the bathroom. To reach the kitchen end, one had to either climb into the trailer and drop down again or step outside through the east door and circle around the rugged exterior of the house.

The adobe house consisted of a half-dozen rooms, each space reflecting both her artistic sensibilities and her pragmatic ingenuity. But Bonnie was never content with mere survival— she dreamed of creating something greater. She took a deeply hands-on role in the construction, personally making and placing each and every block of the adobe exterior walls that she created with a form that would yield just four bricks at a time. It was an arduous task, but as tenacious as she was, she kept going until the house's sturdy walls took shape. Unlike traditional adobe structures that relied on straw for reinforcement, she mixed her bricks from local clay, sand, and bitumen, making them more durable and water-resistant.

Though a man named Abbott Beacham provided substantial help with the house's frame, Bonnie's own hands left their literal mark on the adobe, a powerful symbol of her unwavering resilience and determination.

The house, built around a sturdy wooden frame, was both functional and fortified. There was a reason for that. Out in the desert, miles from any real help, she was vulnerable. She took no chances. Embedded within the walls were gun ports, subtle but deliberate, a reminder that she was prepared to defend herself if necessary. Spike Lynch, who salvaged the scattered remnants of her life from the mud, recalls only this about Margaret Orcutt: "She was a tiny thing, probably four feet seven. A real pistol." Despite her small stature, Bonnie was a skilled shooter. Though she hoped never to rely on that ability, she refused to be at the mercy of anyone—or anything.

She had the workers dig a 14-foot-deep, quarter-mile-long pond, an oasis in the sun-scorched wilderness. She stocked it with fish, its reflective surface a stark contrast to the dry, cracked earth beyond. More than a source of sustenance, the pond was a symbol of her defiance, proof that life could flourish even in the harshest landscapes.

The land itself required just as much ingenuity. A concrete slab on her property, once the foundation for a wooden water tower, became the cornerstone of her water system. She installed a well nearby, drawing water up into the tower, where gravity distributed it across her land. But the desert had its own way of testing resolve. When the well failed, the wooden tank dried out, its seams shrinking in the blazing desert sun until it could no longer hold water. Bonnie, ever resourceful, installed a lawn sprinkler inside, soaking the wood until it expanded once more, sealing the leaks. Eventually, she brought in electricity to power the well, ensuring that water would never be a problem again.

In the conservatory, a baby grand piano hinted at her musical past, its polished surface catching the golden desert light that filtered through the windows. A harp and a cello rested nearby—silent companions to a woman who had once played in orchestras in New York, where music had been as much a part of her identity as the land she now called home.

Despite the rustic nature of adobe homes, Bonnie's kitchen pulsed with life and modern convenience. Propane-fueled utilities and an evaporative cooler offered relief from the relentless desert heat, while the hum of power and the steady flow of plumbing spoke to her ability to bridge the past with the present. Yet, in a quirk of personal habit, she continued to sleep in the small trailer she had first called home upon arriving in the Mojave. Even after the house had been built, the trailer remained her bedroom—a connection with her humble beginnings.

Outside, the desert air carried the scent of sage and mesquite, mingling with the faint metallic tang of brass plaques affixed to plants scattered across the property. Each plaque bore the name of a loved one lost, transforming her garden into a living memorial—a quiet sanctuary where grief and remembrance intertwined with growth and renewal.

It had started with Kenneth.

She had been unpacking a wooden crate when she found it—one of his old brass nameplates, tucked away in a box of tools and paperwork. The sight of it struck her like a blow, the letters of his name catching the light, sharp-edged and unyielding. KENNETH F. ORCUTT. Nothing more. No warmth, no life, just a name carved into metal, as if that was all he had ever been.

She had held it in her hands for a long time, tracing the letters with the tip of her finger, feeling the weight of it. And then, without thinking, she had taken it outside. The mesquite tree by the porch—the first thing she had planted here— seemed the right place. She pressed the plaque into the hard-packed earth at its base, as if anchoring something that had long threatened to drift away.

The idea had grown from there.

In the months that followed, she collected more plaques. Some she had made herself, hammering letters into thin sheets of brass, each strike of the mallet deliberate, measured. Others she ordered from a local metalworker, the names of friends, family, and even long-gone pets etched into their surfaces. With each plaque she placed, she let herself remember.

Her mother's plaque went beneath a wild rosemary bush, its scent thick in the air whenever she brushed past. A childhood friend's name rested in the shade of a desert willow, its pale pink blossoms swaying in the wind. Even the chinchillas they had once bred found their place among the garden's stones, tiny markers tucked between succulents and sage.

But it was Kenneth's plaque she lingered at most. She often found herself kneeling beside it, running her fingers over the weathered brass, speaking to him in whispers the desert winds carried away. Did he know how much she had sacrificed to stay afloat after he was gone? Did he know how often she had been angry with him, how she had cursed his name in the dark of night, only to wake with the bitter taste of regret?

The desert, in its quiet, had become her confessional. She had come here to escape—to disappear—but instead, she had built something. Something that, for all its sorrow, was also a testament to love, to memory, to the persistence of life even in the harshest of places.

And when the wind stirred, rattling the mesquite branches and carrying the scent of sage across the land, she liked to believe it was him answering back.

Bonnie's vision extended far beyond her own comfort. She saw her land as more than a retreat; she dreamed of a sanctuary, a place where others could find solace in nature's quiet embrace.

They say one gives what one did not get. Perhaps that was true for Bonnie. The loss had shaped her—first Kenneth, then her father, then the life she had once imagined for herself. Grief had been a constant companion, but instead of succumbing to it, she turned outward, pouring her energy into creating something larger than herself. A refuge, a sanctuary, a place where others could find what she had been denied—security, stability, a second chance. Whether it was a home for unwed mothers, a retreat for the weary, or simply a place where the desert offered solace instead of solitude, everything she built carried the imprint of what she had lost. If she could not rewrite her own past, she could at least give to others what the world had taken from her.

The desert, vast and untamed, had always been seen as a place of extremes—of isolation, of hardship—but Bonnie sought to redefine it, transforming the barren expanse into a place of refuge, renewal, and even beauty.

Her circular driveway, likely constructed with the same resilient materials as Memorial Drive, whispered of her ambition. More than just a functional necessity, it was a statement—an elegant, deliberate path leading into the heart of the haven she envisioned. At its center stood drinking fountains, ingeniously cooled with crushed ice set in concrete pits, offering visitors a rare luxury in the relentless heat of the Mojave. It was a small but significant gesture, a testament to her deep-rooted belief in hospitality, in providing respite even in the harshest of landscapes.

But Bonnie did not stop there. She was determined to bring life to the desert, coaxing beauty from the earth itself. She nurtured orchids in the arid soil, a feat few would have dared attempt. These delicate blooms—symbols of refinement and exotic splendor—were an unlikely sight in such a harsh environment, yet under her care, they thrived. It was an act of defiance against the elements, a quiet rebellion against the notion that life could not flourish here. With the precision of a scientist and the patience of a gardener, she devised methods to diffuse the sun's scorching heat, using fluorescent tubes to filter and soften the light. Each orchid that bloomed was a victory, proof that determination could bend even the most unyielding forces of nature.

At the center of the lake, Bonnie created a small island, a sanctuary within a sanctuary. Here, she raised chickens, allowing them to roam freely in a protected haven, far from predators and the harsh desert conditions. The island was a self-contained world of its own, a thriving ecosystem that reflected her deep respect for nature and her ability to shape the environment without destroying its spirit.

As Michael Lofy, senior transportation surveyor, later remarked, Bonnie had built "her own kind of empire out there." A woman alone in the Mojave, she crafted a world on her own terms—one of defiance, of vision, and of unwavering purpose. Where others saw desolation, she saw potential. Where others saw limitations, she saw possibilities.

CHAPTER 6

THE HIGHWAY THREAT

The first time Bonnie heard about the highway, it was from a traveler—a man passing through, stopping at the well near her home to refill his canteen. His voice was easy, untroubled, as if he were commenting on the direction of the wind.

"I heard they're building a road out here," he said, shaking the canteen to gauge its weight. "Some kind of highway. Big project. Gonna cut right through the desert."

Bonnie had only offered a slight nod, more out of habit than belief. She had lived in the desert long enough to know that men were always making plans, sketching lines on maps, and dreaming up ways to tame the land. And more often than not, the land won. The desert had its own way of deciding what stayed and what was swallowed whole, turning grand visions into nothing more than dust and forgotten words.

But then, days later, the words came again—this time from her neighbor, a woman who lived miles away but still close enough to share the kind of news that spread through places like this. They were sitting on Bonnie's porch, the air thick with the scent of warm earth and sage, the sun dipping low, stretching the shadows long across the sand.

"I've heard talk of a new highway," her neighbor said, stirring sugar into her tea. "Could bring more people out this way. Might even be good for business."

Bonnie kept her expression neutral and tilted her head slightly, eyes narrowing at the horizon where the last light was slipping behind the mountains. She sipped her tea before answering, as if weighing the words on her tongue.

"Maybe," she said finally. "But good for whose business?"

A highway. Here. She let the words settle and tried to absorb them without letting them take root. Change had come for the rest of the world, twisting cities into something unrecognizable, stirring unrest and uncertainty. But here— here, the desert had held firm. It had been her refuge, her silence. And now, even that was under threat.

Her neighbor chuckled, the sound light but not without tension. "Yours too, maybe. That model kit idea of yours. More folks passing through might mean more folks buying."

Bonnie didn't smile. She tapped her thumbnail against the rim of her mug, a dry metallic click that blended with the chirp of crickets and the distant rustle of wind through the mesquite.

"More folks passing through also means more folks not staying," she said. "And the ones who do?" She paused, then looked her neighbor in the eye. "Not everyone comes out here looking to build something. Some just come to take what they can carry and burn the rest."

The porch fell quiet for a moment. The neighbor watched her stir the last swirl of dust from her cup.

"You don't think it'll happen?"

"I think," Bonnie said, "they'll draw their lines and stake their signs, and the wind will bury it all just like it always does. I've seen plans come and go. The desert doesn't change for talk. It changes when it's ready."

The neighbor leaned back in her chair, studying the sky as it deepened into violet. "Still... would be something, wouldn't it? A real road."

Bonnie didn't answer right away. She looked out past her property, past the trailer-turned-bedroom, past the low adobe walls she had raised by hand. Her voice, when it came, was quiet.

"If they do build it, they'll cut through this place like it's empty. Like no one ever lived here. No one ever loved it."

She set her mug down with finality.

"And they'll be wrong."

The rumors didn't fade. If anything, they grew louder, like a rising tide. A brief mention in the newspaper. Strangers passing through, speaking of surveyors marking the land. And then, one afternoon, she heard it—a distant, rhythmic hum carried on the wind. Not a trick of the desert. Not a ghost of some long-gone time. This was real. Machinery. Progress.

Her chest tightened as she listened, her pulse steady but alert, the same way it had been the day she received the telegram about Kenneth. That same sense of something shifting, something irreversible.

And then, a few days later, her fear materialized. The envelope arrived, thick and official, its return address stamped with the name that sealed it all: Bureau of Land Management. She didn't need to open it to know what it would say.

For a long moment, she stood at her table, the letter heavy in her hands. The world had come knocking. And this time, it wasn't going to turn back.

She didn't need to open it to know what it would say. The world had finally traced its lines all the way to her door.

Bonnie stood at her kitchen table, the envelope resting in her hands like a stone—too heavy, too real. Outside, the wind stirred the edge of the roof with a low, hollow sound, as if the desert itself were whispering a warning.

She set the envelope down. Walked away. Then returned.

She ran her fingers along the crease without tearing it open, letting the tension rise, fill the room, and press against her ribs.

A flash of memory came unbidden—the knock at her door before she was told that her dear husband was no more. The silence that had followed. The way her body had gone still, even as the world kept turning.

Now, standing in the middle of the home she had built with a purpose, she felt that same stillness. But beneath it, a slow-burning heat was rising. Not fear. Not grief. Something harder. Older. Anger, maybe.

Or the cold clarity of knowing you have something to protect.

They were coming for her land—not with shovels or guns, but with paper and ink. With easements and eminent domain and the smug confidence of men who had never stayed long enough to understand what the desert speaks.

Her jaw tightened. Let them try.

She exhaled slowly, then turned and walked across the room. If they thought she would stand by and let them carve up her land without a fight, they were mistaken.

Bonnie reached for her typewriter.

CHAPTER 7

THE FIGHT BEGINS

The letter was the first strike—a measured blow, delivered not with fists but with ink and paper. She addressed the first letter to Mr. Harmon, the Caltrans District Director, laying out her case with the precision of a carpenter fitting joints. The new highway, its wide, merciless sweep of asphalt, would sever her from the world. Her driveway—her artery to life beyond these sunbaked acres— would be swallowed whole, leaving her stranded on an island of dust and memory. It was not simply an inconvenience. It was a disruption to the life she had built, a quiet undoing of the foundation she had laid stone by stone, dream by dream.

Dear Mr. Harmon,

The planned highway construction will cut off my sole access road, leaving my home and livelihood stranded. This land is more than just

property—it is a place of purpose. I have spent years developing a refuge, a place that serves not only as my home but as a sanctuary for those in need. Without proper access, this vision will be shattered, and I will be left isolated, unable to maintain my work or even secure the necessities of life. I implore you to reconsider. Surely, a solution can be found—one that allows progress without erasing the livelihood of those who have built their lives here.

Sincerely,

Mrs. Margaret Orcutt

Newberry, CA

When the response came, it was as she expected. A polite dismissal, words arranged neatly like a wall of bricks with no gaps to slip through.

Dear Mrs. Orcutt,

We understand your concerns regarding the highway project. We deeply value the contributions of residents like yourself. However, the Interstate 40 initiative is vital for California's economic future, and its route has been finalized after extensive planning. We appreciate your understanding as we move forward with this necessary improvement to California's infrastructure.

Sincerely,

Conrad Harmon,

District Director,

California Department of Transportation

Progress. A word as blunt as a bulldozer's blade, indifferent to what it flattened. But Bonnie was not one to step aside.

If Mr. Harmon would not listen, perhaps the governor would. She sharpened her resolve and her words, penning another letter—this time to Governor Edmund G. Brown. She told him about the land, about the sanctuary she had carved from the desert's silence. She spoke of her vision—not just for herself, but for others. The maternity home she had dreamed of, the refuge she had hoped to create. This place was not a relic of solitude but a foundation for something greater. To erase her access was to erase the possibility of what could be.

Dear Governor Brown,

I write to you not simply as a citizen but as a woman fighting to protect what she has built. The new highway will sever my land from access to the outside world, destroying not only my home but the future I have been working toward. This is not just an inconvenience; it is a matter of survival. I have long envisioned a sanctuary here—a home for unwed mothers, a place of solace and renewal. This project, if left unchanged, will erase all of that. I appeal to your sense of justice and community. Surely, there is a way to move forward without burying lives under concrete.

Sincerely,

Mrs. Margaret Orcutt,

Newberry, CA

Bonnie folded the letter carefully, sealing it with the weight of her conviction. She had built this life with her own hands—brick by brick, beam by beam—and she would not watch it be severed without a fight.

The wind picked up outside, rustling the mesquite branches, scattering grains of sand against the windowpanes like whispers. She watched as the sky darkened, the stars beginning their slow emergence. The desert had always been a place of survival. Bonnie intended to prove that once more.

The reply came weeks later, brief and impersonal.

Dear Mrs. Orcutt,

Thank you for reaching out regarding the highway development near your property. While we recognize the impact of infrastructure projects on local residents, the necessity of statewide transportation improvements must take precedence. We regret that we cannot provide assistance in this matter, but we appreciate your civic engagement and concern for your community.

Sincerely,

Governor Edmund G. Brown's Office

Sacramento, CA

A second door closed. But Bonnie had never been one to wait for permission. If the state would not listen, perhaps the land itself could speak through her.

She turned to another letter, this time to the Director of the Bureau of Land Management, pleading not just for her home but for the Mojave itself. She wrote of the fragile desert ecosystem, of the way the highway's sprawl would scar the land, of the ancient creosote and the burrowing owls, of the quiet resilience of this place that had offered her refuge when she needed it most. If they could not see her, then let them see the land and recognize what was at stake.

Dear Director,

The Mojave is a place of rare and irreplaceable beauty. Its land tells stories older than any of us. Its silence holds wisdom that should not be disturbed. The highway project threatens more than just my home—it threatens the delicate balance of an ecosystem that has endured for centuries. I urge you to consider the environmental consequences of this development and to take action to protect this land from irreversible damage.

Sincerely,

Mrs. Margaret Orcutt,

Newberry, CA

The response came after a week, phrased differently but carrying the same rejection.

Dear Mrs. Orcutt,

We appreciate your concerns regarding the environmental impact of the highway project. However, after careful review, the Bureau of Land Management has determined that the proposed construction does not present significant environmental risks under current regulations. We thank you for your advocacy and remain committed to responsible land management.

Sincerely,

Director of the Bureau of Land Management

Another carefully worded dismissal. But Bonnie was not finished.

She sent letters to local assembly members, county supervisors, and anyone whose name she could put on paper. Each letter carried the same plea, and each reply echoed the same indifferent refrain. No exceptions. No reconsideration. The highway would be built, and the world would move on, indifferent to the woman left behind in its wake.

Bonnie set the last letter down and exhaled slowly. She closed her eyes and let herself remember Kenneth's voice, steady and sure. The way his hands had once sketched blueprints for a future they never had time to build. He would have told her not to give in, not to bow to the weight of what seemed impossible.

As dusk settled over the desert, Bonnie stepped onto her porch, the sky bruised with purples and golds. A soft clatter drew her gaze to the gate, where a small group had gathered— Tom Granger, Cora Reynolds, the Martins, and others, their silhouettes sharp against the fading light. They carried lanterns, their glow flickering like stars brought low, and a bundle of handwritten notes tied with twine. Cora stepped forward, her voice steady. "These are from folks down the road, Bonnie. We are with you." Bonnie's chest tightened, the weight of their faith anchoring her. This was no longer her fight alone; the desert had woven them together, their voices rising like the wind, unyielding and fierce.

The next morning, a young girl from the Reynolds' ranch left a painted stone on Bonnie's doorstep, its surface marked with a single word: Hope. Bonnie held it, its cool weight a promise. Her neighbors—scattered across the Mojave's vastness—had become her army, their quiet gestures of defiance as enduring as the creosote. With their support, she would face the bulldozers, the bureaucrats, the endless rejections. The highway might come, but it would not silence them.

The wind outside was unrelenting, and Bonnie's thoughts drifted to the Mojave warriors. They had faced overwhelming odds, fighting against an enemy far larger and more powerful than they could ever have imagined. But they had fought with everything they had, determined to protect their land from being taken. Bonnie felt a connection to them, as though the desert carried their spirit in every gust of wind. She was fighting a different kind of battle, but the stakes felt just as high.

Her thoughts turned to the world beyond the desert. The news was filled with images of the Vietnam War, soldiers fighting in far-off jungles, and young men being sent to their deaths. At home, the streets were filled with protesters demanding change—civil rights, equality, an end to the violence. It was a country at war with itself, and the government seemed more distant than ever, concerned only with battles fought far from the lives of people like her.

The desert seemed to offer no solace in times like this. She had come here to escape the noise of the world, but now, the world was closing in. The Federal Highway Act, signed by President Eisenhower years earlier, had been celebrated as a marvel of progress. It was supposed to connect the country, make life easier for people by creating fast, efficient roads. But to Bonnie, it felt like progress was being paved right over her life, crushing everything in its path.

CHAPTER 8

WRITING TO THE NATION

The next day, the typewriter's keys struck the paper like hammer blows against stone—deliberate, unrelenting. The words came with the weight of the desert wind, shaped by time and necessity.

Dear Senator Thomas Kuchel,

I write to you not only as a resident of Newberry but as a steward of a land that has given far more than it has taken. The Mojave Desert is not an empty expanse waiting for progress to claim it; it is a breathing, enduring testament to time itself, sheltering creatures and landscapes found nowhere else in the world.

Yet, the stakes have been driven. The asphalt ribbons are unspooling. Interstate 40 threatens to carve through this fragile wilderness, severing not only my home but the quiet symphony of life that thrives here—creosote bushes whispering their secrets, jackrabbits darting like shadows, the watchful eyes of burrowing owls standing sentinel in the dusk.

I have written to the California Department of Transportation. I have petitioned the Bureau of Land Management. Each response has been the same—progress cannot be paused, altered, or reconsidered. But what they call progress, I call desecration.

I appeal to you now, as a representative of this land, to listen where others have dismissed. The Mojave does not ask for much. It does not demand, it does not wail—it endures. But endurance is not the same as invincibility. I implore you to act before the machines come, before the unyielding roar of engines replaces the silence of the desert. Once this land is gone, it is gone forever.

Sincerely,

Mrs. Margaret Orcutt,

Newberry, CA

Bonnie rolled the letter from the typewriter, letting it rest in her hands as she traced the ink with her fingertips. How many letters had she written? How many pleas had been cast into the wind, only to vanish like footprints in shifting sand? But this letter—this one carried something different. Not just urgency, but finality. The stakes were no longer hypothetical.

Word had reached her of the construction crews inching closer, their trucks rolling through the desert like invading beasts. The stakes in the sand, once mere wooden markers, now stood like gravestones for a land soon to be buried beneath concrete. They were no longer symbols of possibility but inevitability.

Bonnie drove to the post office, the letter tucked in her purse. Overhead, the sky stretched wide, unbroken, as if refusing to acknowledge the coming change. She thought of Lady Bird Johnson, of the Highway Beautification Act soon to be signed into law. A promise to preserve the untouched beauty of America's landscapes—yet here was this road, cutting through the Mojave's heart, a wound disguised as progress.

She had chosen this life for a reason. When the city had become too loud, too suffocating, she had fled to the desert, where silence was not emptiness but a language of its own. The land had healed her in ways she never thought possible, offering her solace

71

when the rest of the world had felt unbearable. And now, it was her turn to return the favor.

After posting the letter, she returned home. Stepping outside of her car, she listened to the wind. This was no longer just about her home. It was about defending the very spirit of the land, of the life it had sheltered for millennia. It was about proving that silence was not consent. It was about proving that some things, no matter how small in the eyes of men, were worth fighting for.

Weeks passed, and silence answered her. The stakes in the desert grew closer, like a slow march toward inevitable ruin. But then, the winds shifted. California's political landscape changed, ushering in a new senator—George Murphy, a man whose past as an actor meant he knew how to capture an audience. Perhaps, she thought, he would listen where others had dismissed her. Perhaps he would see that her fight was not just about land, but about legacy.

She sat down once more, the crisp paper waiting, and began again.

The desert air carried whispers of war and unrest. Beyond the quiet vastness of the Mojave, the world was unraveling. Protests raged against Vietnam, cities swelled with tension, and people began fleeing to the desert, seeking refuge from a country in turmoil. Bonnie could feel the shift even here, though her battle remained a solitary one. Her war was not fought in the streets but in the steady clatter of a typewriter, in the ink that refused to dry without a fight.

Dear Senator George Murphy,

I write from Newberry, where the Mojave's heart beats beneath my feet and where Interstate 40 threatens to silence it. This highway will sever my only road, stranding my home and the dreams I've built since losing my husband a decade ago. I am no stranger to loss, but I refuse to lose this place—a sanctuary I've crafted not for myself alone, but for others. I envision a maternity home for unwed mothers, a haven where the desert's quiet heals. I run a small business, the Littlest Lumberyard, employing neighbors to craft dollhouses that spark joy. These are not mere plans— they are lifelines for a community you've sworn to serve.

The Department of Transportation and Bureau of Land Management have turned away my pleas. I ask you, as a voice for California's forgotten corners, to intervene. Ensure my access is preserved, not with promises, but with action. The Mojave's people—its workers, its dreamers—deserve a senator who fights for them. Will you be that voice?

With resolve,

Mrs. Margaret Orcutt,

Newberry, CA

Mailing the letter to Senator Murphy, she knew she was running out of options. The stakes in the sand were no longer markers of where the highway would go—they were a countdown, a silent ticking that only she seemed to hear.

The wind picked up as she walked back to her house, carrying the weight of something inevitable. If this letter, too, was ignored, she knew what she had to do next. The road to the White House was long, but if that was where she had to go, then so be it.

A few days later, the rumble of machinery shattered the desert's stillness. Bonnie had heard the noise before, distant and uncertain, but now it was undeniable. The bulldozers had come. Not just to mark the land but to tear it apart.

From her porch, she watched as the dust rose in thick clouds, the earth breaking beneath the weight of something unstoppable. The air, once filled with the soft hum of the desert, now trembled under the growl of engines. This was not a future she had chosen.

Her fight had reached its tipping point.

Dear Assembly Members,

I write to you with a sense of urgency I can no longer afford to contain. Interstate 40 is no longer a proposal—it is a reality. The land is being torn apart, and with it, the fragile balance that has existed here for centuries.

My home is on the verge of being lost, but more than that, an entire way of life is at stake. The Mojave is not a barren wasteland—it is a sanctuary, a landscape that breathes, that shelters, that has given so much and asked for so little. This highway will rip through its heart, displacing its creatures, severing its solitude, and erasing what cannot be rebuilt.

I have petitioned, I have pleaded, and still, I am met with indifference. But I refuse to be ignored. I implore you, as an elected representative of this state, to stand against this destruction before it is too late.

Sincerely,

Mrs. Margaret Orcutt,

Newberry, CA

Bonnie folded the letter, sealing it with the weight of every battle she had fought. The desert wind howled as she thought of posting the letter the next day.

If this letter did not reach the right hands, she would write another. And another. Until there was no one left to ignore her.

Time was slipping away, but Bonnie was not done fighting.

The life before the desert felt distant, like a half-remembered melody—something once clear, now softened by time. Bonnie had once lived in a world of music, of bustling towns and quiet evenings spent at the harp. There had been dreams then, too—ones she had built with Kenneth, ones that had scattered like sand in the wake of his death.

But the desert had given her something back. It had healed her, offering her a place to begin again, a refuge from a world that no longer felt like her own. And she would not let this new life be torn apart. Not now. Not without a fight.

The letter sat on her desk, fresh from the typewriter. She had written to California State Assembly members before, but this time, the stakes felt higher. With the construction machinery now a constant presence in her life, she knew she was running out of time.

The wind outside howled, swirling the desert dust as if the land itself was rebelling against the intrusion. Bonnie walked to the window and peered out, her heart heavy. It wasn't just the construction that troubled her—it was the sense that she was being ignored. No one seemed to care about the destruction of the desert or her home. Her letters fell on deaf ears, her appeals lost in the bureaucratic machine.

But then, a glimmer of hope appeared. As Bonnie went back to the post office one afternoon, she found a letter waiting for her. She slipped it inside her purse and returned home. Once home, she tore it open and read the words carefully—an assembly member had responded.

The letter was cautious, but it was something. It acknowledged her concerns and promised to look into the matter. It wasn't the victory she had hoped for, but it was a sign that someone, somewhere, was listening.

Bonnie folded the letter and placed it on her desk. For the first time in weeks, she felt a flicker of hope. Maybe this wasn't over. Maybe, just maybe, she could still win this battle.

***

The world beyond the desert pressed in from all sides. The Vietnam War raged on, and the protests against it had reached a fever pitch. People were fighting for justice in all corners of the country—whether it was civil rights, anti-war protests, or the growing unrest with the government. Bonnie couldn't help but see the parallels between her own struggle and the larger fights happening across the nation.

The country was divided, and though she was far from the chaos of the cities, the weight of the world felt heavy on her shoulders. People in Los Angeles and San Francisco were moving in search of peace, some even coming to the desert to escape the turmoil. But even here, peace seemed elusive.

The highway was part of that change—bringing the noise, the chaos, the unstoppable march of progress to her doorstep. Bonnie felt the tension of the times reflected in her own life. The desert, once a sanctuary, was now a battlefield.

With each day that passed, Bonnie knew she needed to take her fight to the next level. The construction crews were growing bolder, moving closer to her property, and the noise of the machinery was no longer a distant hum—it was a constant roar, filling the air with the sounds of progress.

She sat down at her desk once more, this time drafting a letter to First Lady Lady Bird Johnson and President Lyndon B. Johnson. Bonnie had followed the First Lady's efforts to protect the country's natural beauty, and if there was anyone who might understand, it was her.

Dear First Lady Lady Bird Johnson,

Realizing your love of beauty, I am taking the liberty of writing to ask your kind help.

In simplicity, my problem is to protect my ranch (a Wild Game Refuge, surrounded by one-thousand-year-old Honey Mesquite Trees) from being land-locked, fenced off and thus destroyed by the projected Interstate 40.

The Right of Way Agent offers but a small condemnation settlement, or, a damage settlement with no way in or out.

I am not disputing Interstate 40's right to take eighteen and one-half acres off of my southern boundary at a satisfactory purchase price; I only want what I have at present: a road on and one off of the present Highway (66).

79

I am planning employment for many people out here in a fenced-in, orderly and quietly beautiful plant area on this place.

The three small pictures can perhaps give you a tiny idea of what I have been able to accomplish thus far.

I have written to your husband also this day, in the belief that perhaps you two are the only ones who have the power to help. In gratitude, I remain,

Sincerely,

Mrs. Margaret Orcutt,

Newberry, CA

January 13, 1965

Bonnie sealed the letter and held it for a moment before she began writing to the president.

Dear President Johnson,

Please forgive this intrusion into your busy life.

The article in the January 11, 1965 Issue of U.S. NEWS & WORLD REPORT entitled, "LBJ's Plan to Beautify America", is so practical and timely that it. seems you may have understanding and know-how with regard to my own related problem.

Several years ago, I purchased this 100-acre panhandle into a government desert-wilderness area with the understanding that the projected Interstate 40 was expected to be laid out south of me and of the present Route 66.

About a year and a half ago, a Highway Aerial Survey was made which has resulted in concrete markers being placed in my southern boundary stripping off from my ranch an area 300 feet wide and over 1/2 mile long. In as much as this bordered a 125-foot, gas-pipe-line right-of-way (Picture #1) through my land, I had planned on making this strip into a beautiful, 100-unit, desert-retirement home for senior citizens.

Such expectations are now down the drain; nor am I disputing the Highway's prerogative. My problem is divided into two:

1) Please note that in Picture #1, Interstate 40 (scheduled to take in the lower 1 inch of this picture) is to go through a grove (only partially shown in Picture #1) of 1,000-year-old Honey

Mesquite Trees, which, once buldozed out, will never be again for us. The ordinary individual, ignorant of their antiquity (some have ground branches over 100 feet long) and rarity now even in this valley, would brush them aside as of no importance. Altogether, there are about 46 of them in the Interstate 40 pathway. If only, the greatest number possible can be saved with perhaps a road sign stating their age, and as such, our National Heritage.

2) At present, I can get in and out by my own 2 legal roads (one on the section line; the other, down the mid section) going onto Route 66. The projected Interstate 40, in addition to taking my land, wants to fence me out entirely --offering either a minuscule condemnation settlement, or, a damage settlement.

It is you who I believe can offer a solution that is in the best interest of both the citizens and the government.

Sincerely,

Miss. Margaret Orcutt,

January 13, 1965

This was her last, best hope. If anyone could understand, they would be the President and Lady Bird Johnson.

The construction crews were closer than ever. The stakes in the ground were no longer just markers of progress—they were markers of time, counting down to the moment when her home, her land, and her dreams would be swallowed whole.

As she walked outside, the desert stretched before her, golden under the setting sun. The battle was not over yet, but Bonnie could feel the weight of it pressing down. She lifted her gaze to the horizon, where dust rose in the distance, and knew that soon, she would have to make a choice.

CHAPTER 9

THE DESERT DOESN'T FORGET

Bonnie sat at the kitchen table, the letter trembling in her hands. The envelope had been creased in the journey, bearing the weight of miles and miles traveled, but its contents felt heavier still. Her name was printed in a formal, unwavering script—Bonnie Orcutt—etched in the ink of a machine, yet somehow, it still carried the gravity of a voice that had reached across the country to speak directly to her.

She unfolded the paper, its crispness betraying its importance, and read.

President Lyndon B. Johnson had acknowledged her struggle, her endurance, and her grief. He had read her words, traced the sorrow embedded in them, and sent her back his own. She let her eyes move slowly over the sentences, absorbing the weight of each phrase, each breath of sympathy and restraint.

I could not intervene. The words were gentle but final. *The federal hand could not reach into the affairs of state governance.* But he had spoken to Governor Brown. He had urged him to act with care and compassion.

Care and compassion.

Bonnie exhaled slowly, pressing her fingers to her temples. The words were meant to soothe, but instead, they lay against her chest like stones sinking into deep water. What was care? What was compassion? Kenneth had been full of both, and yet the sky had swallowed him whole without a moment's mercy. And now, all these years later, she remained a widow fighting a war of paper and silence, all alone.

She thought of Kenneth. Of his hands when they brushed against her cheek. The way he had stood on their wedding day, his eyes full of promises he had never intended to break. She thought of his laughter—warm, rich, and endless—how it filled the empty spaces between words, how it had built a home within her. A home that had burned to the ground the moment his plane went down.

Fate had taken him, and it had taken her, too, in a way. Now, a letter from the highest office in the land sat before her, its words kind but powerless. And yet, somewhere beneath the hollow ache,

85

beneath the exhaustion, a flicker of something else stirred.

Perhaps hope.

She sat for a long while, the letter resting in her lap, staring past the walls of her home, past the edges of her grief, past the years that had tried to bury her. Perhaps, after all this time, she was not entirely lost. Perhaps she could fight just a little longer.

Bonnie woke each morning with the weight of uncertainty pressing against her ribs, an ache that settled into her bones like the desert's chill before dawn. The world outside her window carried on—sunrises still unfurled in rose and gold, the wind still moved through the brush like a whisper of forgotten voices—but inside, time had stalled. She had done all she could. Now, she could only wait.

She fed the birds. She walked the dry earth, toes curling into the sand, feeling the land as if memorizing it with every step. She tended to the things she could control—the rhythm of daily chores, the keeping of small promises to herself. But the silence of the desert gnawed at the edges of her resolve. She imagined her letters stacked in some forgotten drawer, tucked away between matters of greater importance. A widow and her home, a speck on the map, measured against the march of progress.

She had seen it before, the way time and power moved—unstoppable, indifferent.

Her neighbors, sensing the slow erosion of her hope, folded themselves into her days like the wind weaving through mesquite. Tom came by often, his boots leaving prints in the dust as he approached, hands deep in his pockets, a quiet determination in his eyes. "It'll come, Bonnie," he'd say. "They have to listen."

The ladies from town would visit, bringing baskets filled with small comforts—warm bread, fresh peaches, soft cloth they thought might bring her ease. Mrs. Dawson, whose garden grew in defiance of the desert, took Bonnie's hands in her own one afternoon and whispered, "You've stirred something, dear. People are listening. That's more than most can say."

"I'm just trying to hold on. But knowing you're all with me—it's like the desert's got my back."

Still, Bonnie felt the waiting like a hand around her throat. She dreamt of Kenneth in these quiet hours—dreams where his voice was steady and sure, where his presence was a certainty in a world that made sense. She dreamt of him laughing, of him placing his palm against the small of her back, of the sound of his breath just before he spoke. She woke with the cruel ache of his absence and turned her face to the ceiling, as if an answer might be written in the cracks of the plaster.

She wrote again, to the President, in hopes that her concerns would be acknowledged.

Dear President Johnson,

You are handling the Vietnam war situation with courage. Because of which we can guess that your life and the lives of your family have been threatened not once but many times.

On the home front, in many instances the same can be said. I am thinking of the new Interstate Highway System.

Projected Interstate 40 takes in over one-half mile of my ranch and in this connection I would like to commend to your attention a man who has worked under difficulties and harassments; yet, he comes through with vision as well as understanding:

Mr Clyde V. Kane, District Engineer,

CALIFORNIA DIVISION OF HIGHWAYS,

District VIII.

San Bernardino, California 92403

For such men as you and he, we, the
taxpayers, can feel naught but respect
and deep satisfaction.

Sincerely,

Mrs. Margaret Orcutt

Bonnie folded the letter carefully, pressing the creases flat with her palm. She exhaled into the silence of her home, knowing that the fight was far from over. But for the first time in months, she did not feel alone.

That night, she sat by candlelight, pen in hand, but instead of writing, she traced the edges of an old map of Newberry, marking every home, every field, every memory. Each mark was a refusal, a promise— a quiet stand against the erasure of all she held dear. The desert had taught her resilience, had taught her how to bend without breaking, how to endure where others might yield.

The land beneath her feet was not just earth. It was a memory. It was love. It was home. And she would not let it be taken.

CHAPTER 10

A RENEWED HOPE

The knock came at mid-morning; it did not carry the hesitancy of a neighbor or the soft rhythm of a friend. It was a knock that announced itself before a word was spoken.

Bonnie stood at the screen door, a dish towel still in her hand, the scent of lemon soap clinging to her fingers. On the porch stood a man in a short-sleeved button-up shirt, a clipboard tucked beneath one arm, and a badge affixed to his belt like a seal of finality.

"Mrs. Orcutt?" he asked in a voice that carried the weight of memorized lines.

She nodded.

He extended the notice as if it were something fragile, though it had the cold rigidity of steel.

"I'm here on behalf of the California Department of Transportation. This is your formal notice of intent. The state is proceeding with the construction of the highway. You are advised to vacate the property by the date specified."

The sun bore down behind him, casting long shadows across the porch. For a moment, Bonnie didn't take the paper. She stared at it like it was a coiled snake.

"I see," she said, her voice as dry as the wind.

He waited, perhaps expecting a protest or a plea. But Bonnie only took the notice with slow, deliberate fingers. Her hands did not tremble.

He left without another word.

Inside, the paper sat on the table like a verdict. She didn't touch it again for hours. She washed the dishes, fed the birds, and sat in her chair beneath the window where the light fell just right across the floor. But the words pulsed from the table: Notice of Intent. Vacate. Proceed.

They would pave over the desert. Over her and Kenneth's dreams. Over the quiet bones of the life she had built alone. The road would not remember the hands that planted trees or patched screen doors, or traced the outlines of someone sleeping.

Bonnie felt a silence rising—not the peaceful kind that lived in the land, but the kind that smothered. That rewrote.

That night, she pulled out her typewriter and rolled in a fresh sheet of paper as she stared at the blankness for a long time, listening to the desert beyond the walls. Coyotes yipped far off. The wind scratched at the windowpanes like a stray dog looking for warmth.

Then, she began to type.

To the Editor,

For years, I have lived in the Mojave, not as a transient but as one who calls this land home. The state has decided that progress is a straight line carved through the earth, indifferent to the lives it intersects. I am writing to say that this place is not empty.

This land remembers.

It remembers the hands that built our homes, the laughter of children beneath cottonwoods that fought to grow here, the still mornings where the light drips slow as honey across the sand.

I speak not only for myself but for every small voice drowned out by engines of convenience. For every person who has been told their life is in the way.

There is a deeper kind of progress—one that doesn't flatten the past but listens to it. One that asks not just how fast we can go but what we are rushing past. The Mojave is not an empty page for someone else's plans. It is a story already written.

I ask the people of this town, this state, and this country to listen. Not to me, but to the wind that moves through creosote and Joshua trees, to the silence that speaks louder than asphalt ever will. Once the road comes, it does not leave. Once the earth is split, it does not mend.

Stand with me. Not for sentiment but for memory. For meaning.

Sincerely,

Mrs. Margaret Orcutt

When she finished, the paper trembled in the rollers. She removed it gently, holding it up to the lamp. The letters were not just ink. They were a boundary. A refusal.

She sat back and closed her eyes. The desert did not sleep. It held its breath with her. And she knew then: her story had never been just hers. It was the Mojave's, too.

93

She folded the letter carefully, sealing it like a pact. In sending it, she knew she was inviting both sympathy and scrutiny—but also solidarity. She hoped others would see their own battles reflected in hers, that resistance might ripple outward like heat over a salt flat.

The reply from Washington did not come swiftly. Days passed. Then weeks. But Bonnie, stirred by the threat now made real, refused to let the silence thicken.

One morning, after feeding the quail and watering the tomato plants that stubbornly clung to life in their cracked clay pots, she was just stepping back inside when her neighbor called out from across the fence, "I picked up your mail like you asked!" She turned to see him waving a small bundle of envelopes. Thanking him, she walked over, and as she sorted through the stack, sunlight spilled across one envelope in particular. There, in the quiet warmth of the morning, she stood at her doorway and unfolded the letter—from the President.

Dear Miss Orcutt:

President Johnson asked me to thank you for your letter. It was good of you to give him the benefit of your comments and to assure him of your support.

With the President's best wishes.

Sincerely,

Paul M. Popple

Assistant to the President

March 27, 1967

The other response came from Sacramento.

It was nearly midnight when the knock came. Three taps—firm, unhurried. Bonnie, already half-awake from the heat and her own restless thoughts, moved to the door barefoot. Outside, beneath the pale sweep of moonlight, stood a tall man in a dark jacket, the state seal pinned discreetly on his lapel.

"Mrs. Orcutt," he said, doffing his hat. "I apologize for the hour."

She stepped aside without a word, gesturing toward the table where a lamp burned low beside a cup of cold tea. He sat, removed a leather folder, and laid it on the wood between them.

"We'd like to offer a revised settlement," he said. "More than fair market value. Assistance with relocation. Legal help, even. We can have you somewhere quieter, more comfortable, before the ground breaks."

Bonnie said nothing. Her gaze was fixed on the edge of the folder, on the way his fingers drummed faintly against the leather. The night around them was still, the kind of silence only the desert could grow.

"I understand your attachment," he continued. "But this is happening, ma'am. Whether you like it or not. This... is a kindness."

"A kindness," she echoed.

The words lingered in the air. Then she leaned forward, her eyes steady, voice like stone smoothed by years of wind.

"You think you're offering me mercy," she said. "But this isn't mercy. This is convenience dressed up in paperwork."

He looked away, and for a moment, the mask slipped— just enough to reveal discomfort. Maybe even guilt.

Bonnie rose. "I won't sell the bones of my life for your version of comfort. I've buried too much here to leave it behind like an old coat. You tell your people that I'm staying. Let them pave around me if they must."

She opened the door.

The man hesitated, then stood. He nodded once, collected his folder, and stepped into the night.

As the tail lights faded down the dirt road, Bonnie stood in the doorway a while longer. The desert breeze lifted her hair, cool and constant. She felt the weight of her stance settle into her spine like iron. She was no longer just defending a home.

She was defending the right to be heard. And she would not go quietly.

By dawn, she was at her desk again.

This time, she penned an open letter to Governor Brown—addressed through the press. If the private channels had failed, she would let daylight carry her truth.

"Governor Brown," she wrote, "you may not remember me, but I am a woman you once acknowledged. A widow of the Mojave. A keeper of a promise made not just in love, but in law. And I write to you now, not for permission, but for witness."

She wrote of the bulldozers that waited like wolves at the edge of her fence line. Of the meetings, the offers, the veiled threats. She painted a portrait of a government so bent on momentum that it could not see what it trampled.

And then she widened the frame.

"How many others," she asked, "are being written out of their own stories? How many small towns will be erased before the cost is counted in more than concrete and asphalt?"

She ended the letter with a challenge: "Come and see. Stand where I stand. Tell me then if progress is worth the price."

She mailed it to every paper that would print it—from Barstow to Sacramento. The typewriter keys left faint echoes in the early morning air, like the desert itself was taking note.

Next, she wrote another letter to the president.

Dear Mr. President,

Thank you for your early response and for the kind words conveyed through Mr. Popple. I truly appreciate that you took the time to read my letter.

However, my matter remains unchanged. The proposed highway still threatens our home, our land, and the quiet strength of our community. I continue to hope that, upon review, you will recognize how deeply this project affects the lives of ordinary citizens like myself.

With respect and sincerity,

Mrs. Margaret Orcutt

Days passed.

Then a phone call came – from a name she had not heard.

A woman's voice, soft but certain, echoing down the line.

"I read your letter," the voice said. "And I think I can help."

Bonnie leaned closer to the receiver, heart pulsing in her ears. "Who is this?" she asked.

There was a pause. Then:

"Let's just say I know what it's like to be unheard. And I know someone who's listening now."

The line went dead.

Bonnie stared at the receiver in her hand, the silence around her no longer empty, but expectant.

The wind picked up. In the distance, the desert stirred.

CHAPTER 11

THE GATHERING WIND

The morning broke like a whisper—cool and pale, the sky bruised lavender above the sloping arms of the Newberry Mountains. The desert stirred gently, its breath slow and ancient, as if the earth itself had woken to listen. Bonnie stood barefoot on the porch, a chipped mug of chicory coffee warming her hands, its steam coiling into the air like a forgotten song.

Out beyond the adobe wall, creosote and sage trembled in the hush. The wind was tender, not yet burdened by heat, carrying with it the faint rustle of wings—quail darting between yucca shadows, a hawk carving silent arcs above the valley floor. The land, as always, spoke in layers: stillness, then motion; silence, then the low murmur of the coming day.

She had just turned to re-enter the house when the crunch of tires disturbed the morning hush. A government-issued Ford sedan—dust-glazed, incongruous against the golden sand—rolled slowly up the drive, its metal frame groaning with reluctance. Bonnie stiffened, coffee sloshing quietly against the porcelain. Another letter? Another man with polite threats tucked in a briefcase?

The car door opened, and out stepped a tall, slender man in a worn tan suit, his shoes gathering sand like guilt. His tie flapped slightly in the breeze. He paused before approaching, removing his hat as though in reverence—not to her, perhaps, but to the land he was about to trespass upon.

"Mrs. Orcutt?" he asked, his voice low but firm. "David Miller, San Bernardino County. You may have received a call from my secretary."

She said nothing at first, only nodded and gestured to the metal chair across from hers on the porch, the one Kenneth had once favored during early evenings with a whiskey and a map of stars.

"I hope I'm not intruding," he said, sitting cautiously, as though the chair itself might rebuke him.

"You're already here," she replied, placing her mug down. "So I suppose that's a question for the wind."

He gave a sheepish nod, then pulled a small notepad from his jacket.

"I'll come straight to it. The Governor has read your letters. All of them. The one to the Post, the one addressed to him through the press... even the one you wrote to President Johnson. They've made their way through a dozen desks, but they landed where it matters now."

Bonnie didn't speak, her eyes fixed on the hawk overhead, circling like a slow-turning clock.

"He might see you in person," David continued. "Very soon. Says he respects your tenacity. That your words carry more than a complaint—they carry conviction."

A strange quiet fell between them, thick as desert dusk. In the distance, a jackrabbit darted from a mesquite cluster, a flicker of life in a place so often called empty.

"And what does he want from me in return?" Bonnie asked at last, voice steady as bedrock.

David shifted. "Nothing... yet. This isn't a deal, Mrs. Orcutt. It's a conversation."

Bonnie rose, slow and deliberate. The hem of her cotton dress brushed the stone floor the same way her fingers had brushed Kenneth's jaw on the morning of his last flight. She stepped to the edge of the porch, eyes sweeping the horizon.

"Men like your Governor," she said, her voice low and certain, "don't come to the desert unless they want something. Even God waited forty years to bring His people through it."

David offered a soft chuckle, but she didn't smile.

"This land isn't just dirt and sky to me. It's bone and blood. It's my and my husband's dream. It's every brick I mixed with my own hands, every brass plaque I hung on the branches or pressed into the earth beside the plants—each one a promise that the names would not vanish.

She turned to face him, fire low but burning behind her gaze.

"So if he comes here, let him know: I will listen. I will offer him water, shade, and the same patience the desert showed me when I was breaking. But I will not barter memory for pavement. I will not trade grief for asphalt."

David stood, his shoulders sagging slightly under the weight of her words.

"I'll tell him," he said. "And for what it's worth, Mrs. Orcutt... I hope he listens."

She nodded once, the barest movement of her chin, then watched as he returned to his car. The engine sputtered to life and rolled down the drive, leaving only tire ghosts in the sand.

Bonnie remained standing long after the dust had settled. The wind had picked up again, brushing across her arms like a worn shawl. From the porch, she could see the brass plaque beneath the mesquite.

KENNETH F. ORCUTT.

"He wants to meet," she said aloud to the wind, the hawk, the stone, and the bones. "Let him come."

Then, she turned back toward the house.

The Governor's letter had been thin and empty, a polite refusal wrapped in bureaucratic language that barely concealed its indifference. Bonnie had known better than to expect anything else, but still, the dismissal stung like grit caught beneath the skin. She set the letter down on the kitchen table, where it lay like a dead thing, leaching hope from the room.

The days that followed slipped past in a gray, grinding haze. Bonnie moved through them like a ghost tethered to the earth by habit alone—watering the plants, checking the well, writing more letters no one seemed to read. Sometimes, she sat on the porch long after the sun had fallen, the stars flickering above her like distant, silent witnesses. Doubt crept in on those nights, whispering that maybe this fight was too big, too lonely, too impossible.

Still, she endured.

It was later—perhaps a week or two; time had become soft-edged and slow—that another letter arrived. It came tucked between a seed catalog, a faded flyer for a tire sale in Barstow, and a stack of junk mail addressed to "Occupant." Bonnie nearly missed it. She caught the edge of the envelope just as she was tossing the stack onto the kitchen counter.

But the seal stopped her cold.

Thick cream paper, embossed in gold, the return address: **The White House, Washington**. Her hands trembled as she slipped a knife beneath the flap, careful not to tear the page—like a breath held too long, like hope bracing for disappointment.

She paused, the blade stilled mid-seam.

What if it was another platitude? Another polite dismissal dressed in civility? Her heart beat once, heavy. She had written so many letters into silence that the idea of being answered— truly answered— felt almost dangerous. She steeled herself.

She opened the envelope slowly as her eyes skimmed the page.

The White House Washington March 17, 1968

Dear Mrs. Orcutt,

President Johnson has read your correspondence with great interest and concern. He asked that I write to personally acknowledge the thoughtful and compelling nature of your appeal. Your words carry not only eloquence but a sincerity that is deeply moving.

Please be assured that your concerns regarding the proposed highway project through Newberry will be reviewed with the gravity they deserve. The President has directed our team to investigate the matter fully and to ensure that your voice, and the voices of others like you, are not lost in the process of progress.

The President believes strongly in the rights of citizens to be heard and respected, especially when their homes and livelihoods are at stake. Thank you for your courage and your unwavering belief in the value of place.

Sincerely,

Walter Jenkins

Special Assistant to the President

Bonnie read it once. Then again. And again, until the words blurred, until the tears she refused to shed misted her sight like morning fog on sunlit glass.

She sat for a long time at the kitchen table, the letter trembling slightly under her fingertips. Outside, the wind rattled the porch screen, and the hummingbirds flitted in and out of the honeysuckle like messengers of old gods. The land had not changed, but something in her had—a thread pulled taut now hummed with light.

She folded the letter and slid it into a wooden drawer beneath the spice rack. A safe place, between sprigs of lavender and the wedding ring she hadn't worn since Kenneth's last flight.

"Someone listened," she whispered.

A slow, almost imperceptible shift began within her, like the thawing of a frozen river. It wasn't joy, not exactly, but a release. The heavy cloak of doubt and isolation, worn for so long, began to loosen. She rose, the kitchen chair scraping softly against the worn linoleum, and walked to the window.

The sun, now higher, cast long shadows across the yard, illuminating the dust motes dancing in the air. For the first time in what felt like an eternity, she saw not the barren landscape of her grief, but the subtle, persistent green pushing through the dry earth, a quiet promise of renewal.

The letter had come days earlier, and she'd read it a dozen times since, each time tracing the words as if they might shift, vanish, or betray her. But they hadn't. They remained—solid, present, real.

Still, the silence that followed felt fragile. As though the land itself was holding its breath, waiting to see what the state's promises were truly worth.

And then—perhaps a week later, or a little more—came another knock. This one was harder, sharper. Not the hesitant kind delivered by curiosity, but the knock of someone who didn't wait for permission.

Bonnie opened the door to a short man with a buzzed haircut and a state seal clipped to his jacket pocket.

He didn't remove his sunglasses. Didn't smile. "Ma'am," he said, flat and formal, handing over a sealed envelope. "Official notice of execution. Project slated to proceed within sixty days."

She didn't flinch. She only stared at the envelope in his hand, a twin to the first—but colder, like metal in the mouth.

"You've come far," she said, taking it without ceremony, "just to be ignored."

The man gave a shrug, meant to say I only deliver what I'm told. But Bonnie had already turned, her shadow stretching long across the adobe floor as she moved back into the house.

Inside, she opened the notice and laid it beside the letter from Washington.

The two documents sat like rivals—one clothed in steel, the other in light. One full of deadlines. The other, possibility.

She went out to the garden, where the air was thick with sage and soil and the faint metallic perfume of old brass. She knelt beside Kenneth's plaque, fingers brushing the rim.

"They want me gone," she said aloud. "But I'm not a weed to be pulled. I'm a root."

The desert answered with wind—hot now, defiant— curling dust into the corners of her skirt. It lifted the loose pages of a notebook nearby, open to the list she'd once made in the hollow ache of grief.

Build a sanctuary. Raise the lake.

Create a home for women with no place to go.

Be the last to leave.

Bonnie smiled.

They could deliver notices and draw their lines, and pave their plans. But they would never know what it meant to build a life where nothing was given. They would never understand what it meant to bury your love in a place and keep breathing.

She would fight. Not with fists. Not with lawsuits. But with a story. With presence. With the quiet refusal to vanish.

If only President Johnson, with all his power, could hear the whispers of this place, the stories etched into the very soil, she thought, a flicker of hope sparking within her.

Perhaps then, something might change. Perhaps then, someone would truly see. She remembered the tone of the President's secretary, a subtle warmth that had lingered in her ear after the phone call, a hint of genuine concern. There had been a hopeful note in that voice, she mused. Perhaps this letter was not a final word but a beginning. She imagined, in the coming days, another letter, one that would indicate that her voice had been heard, that things were beginning to move in her favor. She imagined him, a distant figure, yet one whose decisions could reshape their world.

That night, she lit a single lamp as she settled into the chair, her fingers resting lightly on the cool keys, but they remained still. She listened, not to the silence of the house, but to the echo of the words she'd read, the confirmation that, even in the vast, seemingly indifferent desert of her isolation, she had been heard. A quiet contentment settled over her, a sense of peace she hadn't felt in years. The need to immediately translate her feelings into words, to fight with the rhythmic clatter of the keys, seemed less urgent. For now, simply knowing that her voice had reached someone, that it had made a difference, was enough. She sat, bathed in the warm lamplight, a silent testament to the power of being seen, of being acknowledged. The typewriter, a weapon, and a solace, remained quiet, holding the potential for future battles, but tonight, it was allowed to rest.

CHAPTER 12

FORCE OF NATURE

The typewriter, faithful and worn, stood at the center of the room like a monument to defiance. Its keys bore the dents of countless battles fought in ink and breath, each letter a volley against the silent, indifferent march of progress. Bonnie sat before it once more, her fingers poised, trembling not from fear but from the steady current of rage and resolve that coursed beneath her skin.

Outside, the desert exhaled a long, slow breath. The brittle creosote bushes shivered under a dry, relentless wind, whispering secrets to the wide, empty sky. The sun, a molten coin nailed high above the horizon, watched impassively as another day bled into twilight. In the distance, the Joshua trees stood frozen in their twisted, praying postures, as if bearing witness to a woman's last plea.

Bonnie pressed her fingertips to the typewriter keys and began.

Dear President Lyndon B. Johnson,

I write to you not merely as a citizen but as a woman standing at the edge of erasure. I have exhausted my appeals to state officials. Their responses, when they come at all, are polished stones—smooth, heavy, and hollow. They speak of necessity, of progress, of things too large and inevitable for a woman like me to stand against.

But I am not merely a woman alone in the desert. I am a steward of this land. I am the echo of those who came before and the guardian of the dreams my husband and I once spun into the very air we breathed.

This place, this humble patch of the Mojave, is more than soil and sand. It is the last living testament to the life we built together—a life now reduced to adobe walls, a half-acre pond, and a field of brass plaques marking love and loss.

If the highway comes, it will carve out my lifeline. It will sever my home from the world. It will bury under asphalt the hopes we dared to plant here.

I appeal to you, Mr. President, not as a bureaucrat but as a man who has known hardship, who has walked the dusty roads of rural America and understood that dignity and dreams are not luxuries—they are rights.

I ask for your intervention. I ask you to see me.

To see this land.

To understand that progress should not demand obliteration.

Sincerely,

Mrs. Margaret Orcutt,

Newberry, California

When she finished, Bonnie leaned back, her shoulders stiff and aching from hours hunched over the keys. The letter sat before her, an offering and a shield both, its words still trembling in the heated air. She folded it with care, slipping it into an envelope and sealing it with the press of her palm—as if imprinting her very soul into the thin paper walls.

She did not dare to hope. Hope was a luxury the desert had taught her to distrust. Still, she would send it. She would send it into the wide, grinding machine of government and pray it might land somewhere a heart still beats.

The wind howled harder that evening, rattling the windows and sending a low moan through the cracks in the adobe. Bonnie stood at the threshold of her home, her arms crossed tightly against her chest, and watched as the desert writhed under the coming dark.

It was then she saw them—two white trucks crawling like pale beetles across the far end of her land, too far to hear but close enough to see the sun flash off their mirrored sides. Surveyors. Again.

The highway's advance had not paused for her grief or her letters. It crept forward with the slow, inevitable hunger of a sandstorm.

Her jaw clenched. Beneath the gentle lines of her aging face, a steel blade of determination glinted sharp.

Inside, the gun portals she had built into her home waited, silent sentinels. At first, they had been precaution— architectural expressions of fear and pragmatism. Now, they pulsed with a different energy. They were not relics of paranoia but declarations of a promise: she would not surrender quietly.

She ran her fingers along the cool edge of the nearest gun port, feeling the rough adobe against her skin. This was not about violence. This was about readiness. About survival. About the stubborn insistence that a woman's dreams were not so easily uprooted, bulldozed, and paved over.

Bonnie stood for a long moment in the gathering dark, the letter to the President still warm from her touch, the surveyors shrinking into the distance, and the great expanse of desert holding its breath with her.

Tomorrow, she knew, the real fight would begin.

The next morning dawned uncertainly, the desert hesitating between light and shadow. The sky, usually a clean wash of blue, was marbled with restless clouds, as if the heavens themselves were uneasy. Bonnie rose before the sun breached the mountains, the house still cloaked in a heavy hush, save for the low rasp of the wind against the adobe walls.

She wrapped a shawl around her shoulders and stepped onto the porch. The desert yawned wide before her, infinite and fragile all at once. She could feel it—something stirring beneath the surface of the day, the way animals sense an earthquake before it strikes.

That was when she heard it: the low, familiar rumble of an engine climbing the dirt track toward her home.

For a moment, her heart gripped tight, imagining surveyors returning, clipboards in hand, ready to measure out her future in cold, indifferent numbers. But as the truck grew closer, she recognized the shape of it—the battered green Ford with a missing hubcap and the figure behind the wheel: Tom Granger, her neighbor from three miles west.

Tom had the look of a man carved out of the desert itself—lean, sun-browned, with hands that spoke in callouses and scars. He swung down from the truck with an easy grace, a wide-brimmed hat shading his weathered face. Bonnie watched him approach, a knot loosening slightly in her chest.

"Morning, Bonnie," he called out, lifting a hand in greeting.

She nodded, wary but grateful for the intrusion. "Morning, Tom."

He climbed the steps two at a time, dust clinging to the cuffs of his jeans. For a moment, they simply stood there together, letting the desert fill the spaces words couldn't reach.

"I heard about the surveyors," he said finally, voice low and steady. "And the letters. You're not alone in this, you know."

Bonnie studied his face. There was no pity there, only quiet solidarity, the kind that grows in hard soil and survives on little more than stubbornness and shared wounds.

"I appreciate that," she said, and she meant it.

Tom shifted, glancing out over the land. His boots scuffed the wooden boards of the porch, a rough, grounding sound. "A few of us got together last night—me, the Martins, old Cora Reynolds. We talked. We don't like what's happening, Bonnie. They're not just cutting through your land. They're cutting through all of us."

Bonnie's throat tightened. She had braced herself for isolation, for the lonely fight she had waged most of her life. She had not counted on the desert answering back through the voices of its people.

Tom pulled a folded piece of paper from his back pocket and held it out. "Petition," he said simply. "We figure if we can't stop 'em ourselves, maybe we can at least slow 'em down. Make 'em hear us."

Bonnie took it, unfolding the creased page carefully. Names lined the sheet—some scrawled in shaky hands, others in bold, defiant strokes. People she barely knew, people who had long kept to themselves, were now lending their voices to hers.

Solidarity, like a hidden spring, had surfaced when she needed it most.

She looked up at Tom, the faintest glimmer of something fierce and luminous burning in her chest. "Thank you," she said, her voice rough with emotion she would not show.

He tipped his hat, modest, as if he hadn't just shifted the weight of the world slightly off her shoulders. "We'll stand with you, Bonnie. You just say what you need."

As he turned to leave, Bonnie watched him go, the green Ford shrinking down the path until it became just another part of the endless landscape. But his presence lingered like the memory of rain on a parched earth.

She went back inside, the screen door groaning behind her. The house, cool and dim, embraced her like an old friend.

The adobe walls rose around her, thick and patient, their very existence a testament to her own hands and will. Embedded within them were the narrow gun portals—slender slits positioned with the precision of a soldier's defense. When she had built them, she had thought of Kenneth, of the dangers he had never lived to see with her, and the deserts, both real and figurative, she now had to cross alone.

The portals were not instruments of violence; they were promises, iron-forged, and earthbound. They were Bonnie herself: small, unnoticed at a glance, but made of something no easy storm could bend or break.

This was her fortress—not a castle on a hill, but a low-slung, sun-battered home crouched against the elements, blending into the desert like a creature that had adapted not out of choice but necessity.

Bonnie ran her fingers along the nearest port's rough edge, feeling the cool press of the adobe under her palm. She imagined the surveyors walking her land, staking their claims with blind hands and blind hearts. She imagined them surprised to find that the woman they had deemed expendable was neither passive nor invisible.

Inside her, the grief that had once threatened to hollow her out had hardened into something far sharper—a blade tempered by loss, sharpened by solitude, honed against the whetstone of injustice.

They would not take this from her. Not without a fight that would leave echoes on the land for generations to hear.

Outside, the wind stirred again, sending the scent of creosote through the open windows, mingling with the faint, sweet breath of the desert's hidden springs. Bonnie stood tall and unyielding, the letter to the President ready to leave in the morning's post, the petition folded like a secret strength against her heart, and her house—a fortress of memory and mud— rising steadily against the gathering storm.

The days stretched thin and shimmering, each one braided with dust, determination, and the iron will of a woman who refused to vanish quietly.

Bonnie's letters multiplied like seeds on the desert wind. Each one carefully typed, each one carrying the imprint of her spirit—a spirit honed by hardship, loss, and a fierce love for the land that had, against all odds, become her sanctuary.

To congressmen and senators, to faceless officials behind marble walls, to agencies whose names stacked like cold stones against her hope—she sent them all. Each envelope was a gauntlet thrown at the feet of progress, each page a line drawn hard and deep into the scorched earth.

Dear Sir,

You hold a pen that can redraw the fate of a land and a life.

Before you sign away my home, I ask you to stand here for one hour. Feel the weight of the sun.

Listen to the silence that hums louder than any engine. Smell the ancient breath of the creosote after rain. Then tell me— honestly—if concrete and convenience are worth the soul of this place.

Sincerely,

Mrs. Margaret Orcutt

Some letters were curt and biting, honed to a blade's edge. Others unfurled like prayer flags, weaving together memory, plea, and defiance. None came back with more than the stilted language of bureaucrats—"We appreciate your concern," "We regret the inconvenience," "The needs of the many outweigh the few."

Nonetheless, the state had offered her options—if you could call them that. One plan placed a towering overpass just beyond her doorstep, a concrete artery meant to preserve access but not privacy. The other was a winding, 4.1-mile driveway, snaking its way from the new highway back to her home like a lifeline drawn in dirt. They had framed it as a concession, a kindness.

Bonnie had learned to read between the lines:

They would not stop for her. They would not see her.

She would have to make them. So, she had chosen the driveway. Not because it was easier—it wasn't. But because she knew what an overpass would bring: strangers skimming overhead, eyes glancing down like tourists at a zoo exhibit. She would not be made a spectacle. Her grief, her history, her hard-won solitude—none of it would be put on display for passing traffic. The desert had given her refuge. She would preserve its silence, even if it meant carving a road through it on her own terms.

One evening, just as the desert was pulling the last tattered light from the sky, Tom's truck appeared again, trailing a comet-tail of dust. Bonnie met him on the porch, a mug of coffee already cooling in her hand.

Tom stepped out, slower this time, his boots dragging with a day's worth of wear. His hat was tucked under one arm, and in his hand, he carried a folded newspaper, edges frayed from handling.

"Got somethin' for you," he said, offering it up like an offering.

Bonnie took the paper, unfolding it carefully. There, buried beneath the brash headlines of wars and markets and scandals, was a small column: **Local Woman Fights Caltrans Over Desert Land Seizure.**

Her name was there. Her home was there. Her fight, once a lonely ripple, had begun to leave circles wide enough for others to see.

Tom shifted, looking out over the vast, darkening stretch of desert. His voice, when he spoke, was low but certain. "We're with you, Bonnie. Don't think folks aren't payin' attention. You're stirring something out here. Reminding us this land doesn't belong to bulldozers and blueprints. It belongs to those who bleed for it."

Bonnie closed the paper and pressed it against her chest, feeling the thrum of her own heart behind the print. A soft, almost imperceptible smile crept onto her lips—not of triumph, but of recognition.

She was no longer standing alone in the gale. The desert itself seemed to rise behind her, not with fury, but with the quiet, ancient strength of roots that run deep and unseen.

That night, under a sky bruised purple with the retreat of day, Bonnie sat again at her typewriter. Her fortress of adobe breathed with the cooling sands, the gun portals casting thin slashes of shadow across the walls. Outside, the coyotes yipped and laughed, a ragged choir serenading the stubbornness of life itself.

She rolled a fresh sheet of paper into the typewriter. Her fingers hovered for a moment—an invocation—and then the first words fell, deliberate and steady, onto the page.

She was not writing for mercy.

She was not writing for permission.

She was writing to remind the world that she was still here—anchored, fierce, unbowed.

Every letter was a stone in the barricade she was building against erasure.

Every letter was a weapon sharper than any blade she could lift.

Every letter was a testament—that a woman, once broken by grief, had shaped herself into something the desert itself might claim as its own.

And though the wind might scatter her words across the sands, Bonnie knew the truth written between every line:

Some battles are not fought to win.

Some are fought so the earth remembers you stood.

CHAPTER 13

THE ROAD TO RESOLUTION

The wind that day carried a softness Bonnie hadn't felt in weeks. It moved differently—less like a warning, more like a whisper. The creosote swayed with cautious rhythm, and the sun, usually a tyrant at midday, cast a gentler light across the adobe walls she had built. She was mending a gate hinge when she heard the engine.

Not the low rumble of a familiar neighbor's truck, nor the roar of a motocross bike testing the cracked ridgelines—but a government sedan, paint dulled by dust. It rolled to a halt just beyond the yucca grove, where the land gave way to gravel and good intentions.

Anchored by place, not praise, she stood in the shade of her porch, arms folded, eyes narrowed. She had learned long ago that the desert would not announce its visitors—it simply delivered them.

The man who emerged was not what she expected. He wore the uniform of bureaucratic diplomacy: pressed slacks, a sun-creased shirt, and a folder tucked beneath one arm like a fragile offering. He moved with the cautious gait of someone who knew he was trespassing—not just on land, but on something older, more sacred.

"Mrs. Orcutt?" he asked, voice hesitant, as if speaking too loudly might stir the dust into disapproval.

She didn't respond right away. Just stared, her silence deliberate.

He cleared his throat. "I'm with the Bureau of Land Management. I was sent to speak with you about... well, about the road."

That word. Road. It had once meant connection, possibility. Now, it meant intrusion and severance. Still, she gestured for him to sit, not as an invitation—more like permission.

They sat across from one another at the scarred oak table, the same one that had held her letters to governors and surveyors, her maps of encroaching lines, and her brass nameplates etched with memory. The air was still, suspended between confrontation and civility.

"There's been a shift," he began, laying out a map that crackled with the weight of decisions. "A proposal. If you agree to allow limited surveying access to certain parcels beyond your eastern boundary... we're prepared to reconstruct your road. Paved. Properly graded. A permanent solution."

Bonnie's fingers twitched toward the edge of the map but did not touch it. Instead, she looked him dead in the eye. "And in return?"

He hesitated. "In return, you cooperate. Allow field access. Environmental assessments. It's not eminent domain, Mrs. Orcutt. It's a compromise."

The word hung in the air like smoke. Compromise.

It was not a victory. But it was not defeat. It was something in between—a clearing in the long, unending forest of resistance.

"I'll review the documents," she said, finally. "Carefully. Word for word. And if there's anything in them that is more than it claims to—if it trades truth for convenience—I'll not sign."

The man nodded, almost with relief. He had come expecting fury. He'd found fire, yes—but controlled, banked, deliberate.

When he left, the road seemed a little less hostile beneath his tires. The wind picked up again, lifting the edge of the map she hadn't yet put away. Bonnie looked down at it, eyes scanning the red ink, the careful lines, the margins filled with small-font legalese.

The desert had taught her patience. It had taught her endurance. And now, it was teaching her the hardest lesson of all: that even the fiercest protector must sometimes consider the treaty—not as surrender, but as a strategy.

The road had returned. But it would do so on her terms.

Another official letter arrived on a Thursday. The envelope was embossed with the words **Sacramento.**

Bonnie turned it over in her hands once, then twice. She didn't open it right away. She placed it gently on the table— her table, the one that had borne the weight of grief, defiance, and ink—and brewed a pot of coffee. Some things deserve a ceremony.

The blade of her letter opener slid cleanly beneath the flap. The paper inside unfolded with the gravity of law, its language laced with cautious dignity. But there it was, in black-and-white, unmistakable:

"The State of California acknowledges the necessity of

preserving access to private property affected by current and future infrastructure development. In light of recent negotiations, we affirm our commitment to reconstructing the access road serving the residence of Mrs. Margaret Orcutt in Newberry. This road will be maintained as a permanent right-of-way, under terms mutually agreed upon and recorded with San Bernardino County."

Signed in careful strokes by the Governor's Chief of Staff.

A promise, at last, that carried the state's weight.

Bonnie leaned back in her chair, the paper trembling slightly in her hands—not from fear, but from the sheer, unfamiliar release of relief. Not a total victory, no. But in a world where the powerful often moved without consequence, where governments sliced through maps like surgeons without anesthesia, this—this was something extraordinary.

She had been heard.

And in being heard, she had become something more than just a holdout on a patch of desert. She had become a crack in the concrete, a space where light broke through.

Word traveled fast in Newberry—not by newspaper, but by porch swings and gas station counters, by the gravel murmurs of desert mail routes. Bonnie didn't announce the news so much as allow it to arrive. The road would stay. Access would be preserved. She had bent the will of the state without yielding her own.

At the local store, a man clapped her on the shoulder with a grin wide as the I-40. "Heard you gave Sacramento a hell of a run for their money."

Bonnie just smiled. "Just taught them how to read a map properly."

Soon, neighbors who had once watched from afar with quiet sympathy began to ask questions of their own: How did you do it? Who did you write to? What laws did you quote?

She shared what she could—names, addresses, clauses. But what she offered most was not strategy. It was proof. Proof that resistance wasn't futile. That the softest voice, when sharpened by principle, could pierce the densest wall of bureaucracy.

She hosted a small gathering in the courtyard by the pond, lanterns strung like starlight across the adobe walls. The chickens clucked softly from their island in the lake, and the mesquite trees whispered approval. She wore her good shoes, the ones with dust in the seams and dignity in the stitching. And she spoke.

Not long. Just enough.

"This land," she said, her voice low but steady, "was never meant to be convenient. It was meant to be loved. And no piece of paper, no bulldozer, no suit behind a desk has the right to take that from anyone."

They nodded, some with fists clenched, others with tears rising. The desert, after all, had taken from them too.

That night, someone asked her if she would leave now, now that the fight was done.

Bonnie just laughed. "Leave? I've just had the road rebuilt. Let them come. I'm staying put."

Her story, like the road itself, wound its way outward. Journalists came. Environmental advocates cited her letters. Civic groups invited her to speak, though she often declined. She wasn't looking for fame—just a little peace. But in standing her ground, she had become something unexpected: a symbol. Proof that the gears of power could be slowed, redirected, even humbled—if enough grit got in the teeth.

The desert had taught her that. The wind, the sun, the silence. All of them had conspired to shape her not into a relic but into a root. Something immovable. Something that endured.

And now, as dusk fell over her land and the headlights of an occasional traveler traced the edge of her new road like a silver ribbon on the sand, Bonnie stood at the gate and watched. Not to see who came or went, but to remember what it cost—and what it proved.

The land was hers.

Not because of ink or signatures. But because she had stayed.

CHAPTER 14

THE DESERT'S KEEPER

In March 1967, the newspapers reported it as an afterthought—just another bureaucratic oddity buried in the proceedings of the San Bernardino County Planning Commission. A town had changed its name, and no one in power had noticed until a resident, Margaret Orcutt, came forward with plans to build a wildlife preserve.

The commissioners were caught off guard. Newberry, it seemed, was no longer Newberry. It was now Newberry Springs. Had they approved this? Had there been some official decree? No, they learned—it hadn't come from them at all. It had come from Margaret, who had simply decided one day that the town should reclaim its original name.

Of course, there had been practical concerns too. Mail meant for Newberry was often misrouted to Newberry Park, California, and vice versa—a logistical nuisance that seemed to validate the change. But it was Margaret's vision, not a clerical error, that gave the name its permanence.

She had walked the dusty roads and knocked on doors, gathering signatures from the scattered residents who called this stretch of the Mojave home. Four-fifths of the registered voters had agreed, signing their names to a petition that she had sent off to Washington, D.C., addressed to the Postmaster General himself.

For a year, nothing happened. The desert was used to waiting.

Then, in a twist both bureaucratic and absurd, the change finally came—not because of her petition, not because of months of quiet persistence, but because she had written a letter to Postmaster General Lawrence O'Brien, thanking him for the department's Christmas stamp. Somewhere between holiday cheer and government red tape, someone must have finally taken a second look at her request. And so, just like that, the town's old name was restored.

The commission, with a shrug and a chuckle, granted her request for the wildlife preserve—forty acres east of town, an eight-foot-deep lake with an island at its center. Good luck to Newberry Springs, they told her, as if the name itself carried some magic, as if, in renaming it, she had breathed something back into the land.

Margaret had not just changed the name of a place. She had willed it into being.

Now older, Margaret Bonnie Orcutt stood at the edge of her land, her boots sinking into the sand she had claimed, defended, and called kin. The Mojave stretched around her, still and eternal, its silence familiar and forgiving. This desert had never bowed easily—and neither had she.

What once threatened to divide her from it—the looming scar of the interstate—had, in time, curved around her property like a reluctant apology. Not without a fight. She had faced down the state and its looming claims of eminent domain, her typewriter pounding out protests that echoed from county offices to congressional mailrooms. When the dust settled, she hadn't just protected her land—she had earned a road. A full 4.1 miles of federally built pavement reached out from her home like a defiant lifeline.

And in time, even those once seen as adversaries became guests. The construction crew, once viewing Bonnie's land as a mere obstacle to progress, came to regard her with quiet awe. The tension of the eminent domain battle, which had pitted her against their bulldozers and blueprints, dissolved into an unexpected camaraderie. The workers' initial wariness softened into genuine fondness once the dispute was settled, their visits to her property marked by shared laughter and stories under the Mojave sun. Among them, the foreman—a licensed pilot with a penchant for open skies—found a particular kinship with Bonnie. He would land his Cessna on the long, straight stretch of her newly paved road, the one locals called "Mrs. Orcutt's Driveway," its asphalt a hard-won testament to her defiance.

On sweltering desert afternoons, Bonnie and her new friend would sit on her porch, the air thick with sage and the faint hum of cicadas. Over glasses of iced tea or lemonade, condensation beading like tiny oases, they'd talk—not just about the road, but about the desert itself, its unyielding lessons, and the strange paths that drew people together across its vastness.

"You know, Mrs. Orcutt," he said one day, wiping sweat from his brow, his Cessna glinting in the distance like a grounded star, "I thought you were just some stubborn holdout. But this?" He gestured to the adobe house, the pond shimmering beyond, the mesquite trees bearing brass plaques. "This is something else. You built a world out here."

Bonnie's lips quirked, her eyes sharp but warm. "And you thought you'd pave right through it, didn't you."

He chuckled, leaning back in the creaking metal chair. "Guilty. But I'll tell you what—this desert's got a way of teaching you respect. For the land. For folks like you who don't bend easy."

She sipped her tea, the ice clinking softly. "The desert doesn't care for your plans or mine. It just is. You learn to listen to it, or it buries you."

He nodded, his gaze drifting to the horizon where the Newberry Mountains stood like silent sentinels. "Kinda like flying. Up there, you're free, but you're nothing if you don't respect the wind. One wrong move, and…" He trailed off, his fingers tracing the rim of his glass.

Bonnie's eyes softened, a flicker of her own loss— Kenneth's plane, swallowed by the sky— crossing her face. "You respect the wind," she said quietly. "I respect the roots. Maybe that's why we're sitting here now."

Yet the desert was never static—and neither was the world beyond it.

In the sun-scorched heart of the Mojave Desert near Newberry Springs, California, the Orcutt's Driveway stretched 4.1 miles, a singular testament to the tenacity of Margaret Bonnie Orcutt. The construction was completed in the summer of 1968. Officially named Memorial Drive, it's known locally as "Mrs. Orcutt's Driveway," connecting her hand-built adobe home to the historic Route 66, just south of Interstate 40 (I-40). The driveway, a narrow, ruler-straight ribbon of asphalt, lies parallel to I-40, its unyielding path carved through the desert landscape. It originates at her property, a low-slung dwelling nestled near a shimmering pond, and cuts due east, terminating at a junction with Route 66, now a quieter shadow of its former self. Its stark linearity, unbroken by curves, mirrors Bonnie's unyielding resolve.

Bonnie felt a surge of pride, the hum of her old Ford pickup blending with the desert's silence, each mile a reminder of her triumph. She'd often pause at the wheel, hands gripping the steering, whispering to her late husband, Kenneth, "I did it, didn't I? You'd be grinning ear to ear." These moments, steeped in memory, infused her with strength, his adventurous spirit—once soaring in planes—guiding her through the fight.

Beyond Mrs. Orcutt's personal victory, the driveway became an unexpected boon for others, its straight, smooth expanse attracting diverse users. In the late 1970s and early 1980s, *Car and Driver* magazine wrote an article about the driveway. They

139

had covertly used it for high-speed car tests, with vehicles like the Banks Power street car breaking the 200-mph barrier drawn by the road's isolation and length.

Now, Mrs. Orcutt's road and house have transformed into a mecca for travelers and Route 66 enthusiasts, drawn by the allure of her defiant stand against the government and her unique desert life. YouTube videos capturing the site have amassed millions of views, fueled by the *Car and Driver* article and the fervor of an "Orcutt fan club," turning her story into a cultural touchstone. Her tale of resilience, set against the 1960s backdrop of social upheaval, resonates with those who see her as a pioneer of independence, her driveway a symbol of a woman who carved her own path in the unforgiving Mojave.

The driveway's existence preserved her vital link to the old highway, benefiting those who still relied on the driveway's fading commerce. Bonnie, watching cars streak by, would muse about Kenneth's love for speed, imagining him chuckling at the irony of her road becoming a racetrack. "You'd have loved this, Kenneth," she'd murmur, her eyes tracing the horizon where the driveway met the sky, feeling his pride in her unyielding stand.

But even as her quiet triumph stretched across the desert floor, change was sweeping far beyond the edges of her land. The same decade that saw Bonnie's driveway repurposed as a desert speedway was also unraveling the fabric of the country she once knew. While she fortified her sanctuary against the winds and time, the world outside was growing louder, more fractured. Headlines no longer spoke of pioneers or visionaries but of unrest and upheaval. The hum of engines on her road felt almost out of step with a nation that was, itself, trying to find direction.

The 1970s had arrived, turbulent and raw. A nation still bleeding from the assassination of President John F. Kennedy was now fractured further by the war in Vietnam. Cities swelled with protests, grief, and cries for justice. Young men were torn from their homes and sent into jungles half a world away. The air buzzed with talk of revolution—civil rights, women's liberation, environmental awakening.

Bonnie felt those shifts like distant thunder in her chest. Though far from the marches and sit-ins, she wasn't untouched. She had seen friends lose sons to war. She had read, with growing ache, the headlines about injustice and loss. But while others sought refuge in cities and movements, Bonnie turned ever deeper into the desert.

The land had taught her how to survive heartbreak. From grief, she had learned resilience.

From uncertainty, determination. The silence of the Mojave became a kind of teacher, shaping her into a woman of the land—self-sufficient, visionary, and grounded. And though she chose solitude, it was never isolation. She had friends across Newberry Springs, Barstow, and even farther afield—people drawn to her warmth, her clarity, her grit.

She had arrived in the Mojave like a pioneer a century too late—an Indiana woman in an Airstream, carving out a life where there was nothing but wind, sun, and stubborn hope. It was easy to picture her in another era, trailing a covered wagon across the plains, drawn west not by gold or fame but by the promise of solitude and space. Before "off-grid" became a buzzword, Bonnie lived it—hauling water, building with her own hands, respecting the rhythms of the land. But she was more than a desert homesteader. She was an early eco-warrior, decades ahead of her time, fiercely protective of the fragile ecosystem around her. She spoke up for the desert tortoise, for the birds that nested near her pond, for the brittle bushes and wildflowers that bloomed defiantly after every rain. To her, the Mojave wasn't empty—it was alive, sacred, and in need of a voice. She gave it hers.

But even in the desert, change was inevitable. It crept in like the shifting dunes—subtle at first, then undeniable. Her stillness was pierced by the growing hum of progress, by whispers that became headlines, and by needs greater than her own. And she answered them the only way she knew how: with action.

She dreamed not just of preserving her sanctuary but of expanding it into a refuge for others. A maternity hospital for unwed mothers. A place of care, dignity, and second chances. She would call it the Cywren Foundation, a name as soft and strong as the women it would serve.

It was bold. Radical, even. But Bonnie had never done things the expected way.

To raise the funds, she turned to the land again. Not with adobe bricks this time, but with speed and dust and spectacle. She staged motocross races—thundering events that transformed her 100-acre property into a proving ground. Riders came from across the state, engines roaring against the desert wind, pushing their bikes and bodies through the dry heat and shifting earth.

It seemed improbable. But improbability had never stopped her. In 1975, the Los Angeles Times reported on her effort to build a motorcycle raceway. A petite, 80-pound harpist with no background in motorcycles had become a land developer, carving a six- to twelve-foot-deep track into the Mojave dust. She had never ridden a bike. She wasn't a fan of the sport. But she needed funds, and dreams demand means.

"I need a great deal of money to fulfill my lifelong dream," she had told those who questioned her. "This seems to be a practical way of raising that money."

Her dream had begun long before Newberry Springs, perhaps even before Kenneth. "I've always had this concern about the high rate of infant mortality in this country," she would say when asked about her strange, unwavering pursuit. "That is why I want to build the research center."

She had no children of her own. That hadn't mattered. She had known loss and, through it, had found purpose.

The raceway, that strange and dusty temple to adrenaline, was meant to fund that purpose. She had transformed the land again, flattening its natural curves into a ribbon of challenge and speed. But fate, as it often did, intervened. An injury postponed the track's opening. The machines fell silent. The riders moved on. The dream waited, but her resolve never wavered.

She had known how to wait. She had come to the desert eleven years earlier, not long after Kenneth's sudden death in a plane crash fractured the world they'd built—the fur stores, the city, the future that never came. Grief had drawn her west, into the sun-scorched silence where nothing expected of her could survive. Now, with the dust still settling from the 1964 highway upheaval, the time felt measurable at last—eleven years of waiting, building, and becoming.

And yet, she built. Her home rose from the sand with adobe-like grace, molded from the very earth she lived upon.

As years passed, her sanctuary grew. Her orchard bore fruit; her pond shimmered under moonlight; her road whispered stories of stubbornness and steel. The brass plaques multiplied—a memorial garden scattered across her land: her mother, her father, Kenneth, even chinchillas once destined for a business that never came to be. She remembered them all. Each name was a promise that nothing is truly gone if it's remembered.

Her typewriter, though quieter now, still answered calls. Letters to newspapers, handwritten notes to the women she sheltered, quiet thoughts tucked into a wooden box. She had become the Mojave's chronicler, a voice for those who could not speak, a steward of the desert's story.

Visitors came. Some were drawn by legend. Some by the glint of her preserves. Some by the need for a story that defied logic. Environmentalists quoted her letters. Journalists chronicled her campaigns. Travelers paused at the edge of her road, as if to step briefly into the orbit of something rare.

Newberry Springs grew, too—its name reclaimed by her petition, its identity shaped by her defiance.

At dusk, Bonnie walked her land. Her steps slower now, but rooted. She carried the years in her bones, the battles in her shoulders, the love in her heart. The plaques would outlast her. The orchard would feed mouths she'd never meet. The road would stretch into history.

She thought of Kenneth. Of her mother's hands. Of medicine, of typewriters, of racing tires and harp strings. Of the desert, which had given her everything she needed—just not all at once.

And she thought of herself—not as a widow, not as a woman out of place in time, but as who she truly was:

Bonnie Orcutt. A force of nature. A pioneer. A keeper of the Mojave.

SOME YEARS LATER

In the sun-soaked expanse of the Mojave Desert
during the early 1970s, George Robinson, a broad-
shouldered Caltrans supervisor standing 5'7" with a
flat-top haircut, roamed the 660 lane miles under his
charge. At 32, George was a desert native, born in
1942, raised on a five-acre ranch where his family
milked their own cow and kept chickens, living a
self-sufficient life that echoed the rugged simplicity
of the land. His career with Caltrans, sparked by his
father's urging to take a physical exam before
finishing high school, had taken him from Desert
Center to Barstow, overseeing stretches like
Highway 58, Interstate 15, Interstate 40, and
Highway 247. It was on one of his routine patrols
through Newberry Springs that curiosity led him
down Hazen Drive, the old name for Mrs. Orcutt's
Driveway, a paved road born from necessity after
Interstate 40 severed the old Route 66, to the hidden
home of Mrs. Margaret Orcutt.

George thought of her as matronly, a woman of about five feet with her hair neatly pinned up, dressed in practical clothes suited for milking goats or feeding tortoises, far from the fancy attire of the woman of that era. Her demeanor was warm and welcoming; she greeted him with a smile, perhaps reassured by the familiar orange of his Caltrans truck, which might have stirred the geese or goats that served as her sentinels. Inside her home, nestled among catclaw bushes and trees that cloaked it from prying eyes, she offered him a glass of goat's milk mixed with chocolate syrup—a surprising and unique treat in the arid desert that he found super appetizing.

For nearly an hour, they talked about the desert's ways, her two or three-foot-long tortoises waddling nearby, friendly when fed, and the goats that sustained her. The scene reminded him of his own childhood, where self-reliance was a way of life.

On his second visit, he brought his family, and once again, Bonnie's hospitality shone through as she served them all goat's milk. Her reputation, as noted by George, was dual-edged: sweet to those like him, yet stern when needed, a grit born of living alone in a harsh land. This toughness had been tested years earlier, between 1964 and 1966, when Interstate 40's construction sliced through her connection to Route 66, thrusting her into an eminent domain battle. Though not directly involved, George had heard the local "scuttlebutt" back then, whispers of a lady fighting the government to keep her land, a fight that ended with her signing away parts of her property under pressure.

The road itself told its own story of struggle. George learned from Mel Halstead, a seasoned Caltrans lead worker in Newberry Springs, that the ground near Bonnie's property was prone to sinking, a problem that plagued old Route 66 and persisted with the freeway. Workers like Robbie Dill, another long-time Caltrans hand in Barstow, had tackled it, applying asphalt or coal mix to cracks annually. Bonnie's driveway had even served as an impromptu landing strip for a private plane, used by Caltrans or project engineers to take soil samples to assess the sinking risk.

George's memories of Bonnie were woven into a broader tapestry of desert life, where community bonds ran deep despite the vast distances.

EPILOGUE

The Mojave does not forget. It doesn't weep or shout—but it remembers.

Bonnie Orcutt's home still crouches in the sand, not a hundred yards from the humming artery of Interstate 40, where cars rush past her broken silhouette without ever knowing her name. Her house, now half-swallowed by time, once stood defiant. Vandals have torn through it—ripping the trailer from its side, cracking the roof open like a chest no longer guarded. The gun ports she carved herself now stare blankly at the highway. They are empty, like the hallways of memory echoing within.

She was the last of her family.

The final breath of a line buried back east. When Bonnie came here, she didn't just settle in the desert— she committed to it. She loved a man who died too soon, dreamed of a place for lost women to find themselves again, and carved her name into the bureaucratic bedrock to force a road into being.

And though that road once roared with speed—test drivers pushing past 200 miles per hour—it no longer invites velocity. The pavement is cracked. The shoulders crumble. It cannot be what it once was. But it remains. It always remains. So, too, does Newberry Springs. The desert tried to take parts of it—homes half-swallowed by dunes just a few miles away— but the town clings on. Not lively, but alive. Gas stations. Markets. And always, Route 66—less traveled now, but still breathing.

Only the ghostly outline of Bonnie's Littlest Lumberyard survives. A few concrete edges where metal garages once stood, long taken down and recycled elsewhere, no doubt by nomadic people perhaps who traveled the highways and byways of a distant America. A square of emptiness where dreams once sat on hand-built shelves. Photographs are scarce. Records are scattered. But every year, YouTubers, bloggers, and wanderers find their way to her ruins. They film. They speculate. They speak her name.

And here, now, this book.

In the Mojave's vast pulse, roads stretch like arteries, carrying the lifeblood of travelers through the desert's heart. For Mrs. Margaret Orcutt, these arteries were more than mere pavement—they mirrored her own resilience, her spirit tethered to the land and to Kenneth, her husband lost to a plane crash. Tragically, her life ended on December 7th, 1986. Aged seventy-seven, she suffered a stroke, a cruel echo of the government's surgical slice through her world two decades earlier. When Interstate 40 severed her connection to old Route 66 between 1964 and 1966, it choked the flow of her existence, much like a blocked vessel. Yet, in a twist of irony, the authorities performed a kind of surgery on the landscape, grafting Mrs. Orcutt's Driveway to restore access to her isolated homestead. This new artery, born of her fierce battle against eminent domain, breathed life back into her desert haven, a testament to her unyielding heart that beat for the Mojave's wild, untamed soul. However, no surgery could save the woman herself.

She spent the final months of her life in a nursing home in Fontana, California—far from the land she had fiercely protected for decades. As her health declined, distant relatives from across the country were contacted. She died on Pearl Harbor Day—quietly, without the desert at her side.

There's a strange irony to the date: a national day of defiance, a moment when America stood its ground, while also marking the end for a woman who had done much the same in her own quiet theater of war. She, too, had her own personal Pearl Harbor moment when assaulted by a power seemingly greater than her and had pushed back against an advancing force, not with weapons, but with a typewriter—and won.

And like so many women of her generation—emerging from the shadows of World War II and the era of Rosie the Riveter—Bonnie understood what it meant to take on work, roles, and burdens the world didn't always see as hers to carry. She brought that same stubborn independence into the fight for her land.

The news of her death rippled through Newberry Springs, leaving a profound sadness among the townspeople. Bonnie, though not a native, had woven herself into the community, her warmth and tenacity earning her many friends who mourned the loss of a woman whose defiance and kindness had shaped their desert home.

She was cremated on Dec 9, 1986, at Crestlawn Mem. Park, Riverside, CA. Her and Kenneth's headstones are located in Earlham Cemetery, Richmond, Indiana. Her story didn't vanish. It left its mark not only in sand and silence but in the stubborn continuity of the place she called home. Newberry became Newberry Springs during her lifetime—a small but telling shift, a nod to the region's character and resilience. While Bonnie didn't rename the town herself, her presence and persistence added meaning to that stretch of desert, quietly embedding her name into the story of the land. It clings—like the Mojave dust to boot soles. Like sun-faded siding that still won't fall. Her life was one long refusal to yield.

Will her home be rebuilt?

Will someone buy the land and raise her mission from the sand?

A cultural site. A refuge. A monument to tenacity. No one knows.

But the sun still rises. The road still runs.

"The desert doesn't survive—it endures, shimmering with the patience to outlast everything built upon it."

Bonnie Orcutt didn't ask to be remembered.

But the land does, anyway.

THE END

WORDS OF WISDOM –
IMPORTANT DISCLAIMER

The stretch of driveway where Margaret "Bonnie" Orcutt made her final stand still exists in the Mojave Desert. It is not preserved or protected. It is just... there—weathered, isolated, and slowly disappearing into the dust.

The author does not own the land, has no affiliation with its current or past owners, and makes no claims of ownership, authority, or access rights.

The property is in a significant state of decay. There are genuine risks present, including unstable ground, debris, desert wildlife, and extreme heat. It is not maintained, nor monitored, and may not be safely accessible. Anyone choosing to go there does so at their own risk. This book is a historical account, not an endorsement or invitation to visit. The author assumes no responsibility for any actions, incidents, or consequences that may result from visiting the property and area.

It is this author and historian's hope that what remains is left undisturbed for the ages to consume without the callous hearts and hands of man or woman doing even more damage. That being said, people get curious, and thousands of respectful and well-intentioned people over the years have visited the property. Sadly, however, many others chose not to show respect or common sense when they visited this formidable woman's property and caused destruction. Don't be like them.

The author is not the property's caretaker, but should you decide to visit, please:

- Remain on public roads and rights-of-way. Be safe and use common sense.

- Do not trespass or disturb the surrounding land.

- Respect the site—take nothing, leave nothing. Honor her history and her legacy.

- Do not damage, graffiti, sticker, tag, or vandalize any part of the home, property or area.

- Drink plenty of water in the desert as the temperature can exceed 110 degrees at certain times of the year.

- And lastly, please be respectful of the community and neighbors. They each live a quiet life in an isolated area for a reason. Visit quietly and respectfully.

This is not a tourist destination. It is a storied site filled with history.

A woman stood her ground here. Honor that moment. She deserves better.

LEAVE A REVIEW

If this story meant something to you, say so. Reviews matter to authors more than you may realize. It's what drives important stories like this one up the charts, and they also help preserve Mrs. Orcutt's memory and carry it forward to others by getting her story out to more people and readers.

Leave a review using the QR code below or at the Amazon link: https://a.co/d/hr5ceXe.

It would be greatly appreciated if you left one on whatever site you found this book, such as Goodreads:

https://www.goodreads.com/review/edit/228586009

KEEP HER STORY ALIVE

Download your Mrs. Orcutt's Driveway commemorative badges suitable for printing on stickers: https://mrsorcuttsdriveway.com/desert-downloads

Check out your Route 66 Desert Passport: https://flipbook.cvwooster.com/route-66-passport#page1

Sign up for historical updates and new discoveries at https://mrsorcuttsdriveway.com

Share your photos using #MrsOrcuttsDriveway

We would love to have you join the *Mrs. Orcutt's Driveway Facebook* group dedicated to her life and story at:

https://www.facebook.com/groups/1027375475811076/

Like what you have read? Here are some other titles by C. V. Wooster

See the full selection at https://cvwooster.com

For readers drawn to gripping historical narratives, *Searching for Bowlby* offers a rare window into the life of a quiet revolutionary. British psychiatrist **John Bowlby** (1907–1990) reshaped the way we understand human relationships. His groundbreaking Attachment Theory transformed parenting, therapy, and education—and continues to influence generations.

Discover the man behind the science in this vivid retelling of a life that changed lives.

Pre-order available now and releasing soon. → https://searchingforbowlby.com

THE ARCHIVE

THE WHITE HOUSE

LBJ presidential library and museum

Margaret Orcutt

Mrs. Margaret Orcutt
Orcutt Desert Ranch
Post Office Box 111
Newberry, California

Orcutt Desert Ranch,
Post Office Box 111,
Newberry, California   92365

January 13, 1965

Dear Mrs Johnson:

Realizing your love of beauty, I am taking the liberty
of writing to ask your kind help.

In simplicity, my problem is to protect my ranch (a Wild
Game Refuge, surrounded by one-thousand-year-old Honey Mesquite
Trees) from being land-locked, fenced off and thus destroyed by the
projected Interstate 40.

The Right of Way Agent offers but a small condemnation
settlement, or, a damage settlement with no way in or out.

I am not disputing Interstate 40's right to take eighteen
and one-half acres off of my southern boundary at a satisfactory
purchase price; I only want what I have at present: a road on and
one off of the present Highway (66).

I am planning employment for many people out here in a
fenced-in, orderly and quietly beautiful plant area on this place.

The three small pictures can perhaps give you a tiny idea
of what I have been able to accomplish thus far.

I have written to your husband also this day, in the belief
that perhaps you two are the only ones who have the power to help.

In gratitude, I remain,

Sincerely,

Mrs. Orcutt

Mrs L. B. Johnson,
White House,
Washington, D. C.

NO OTHER CORRES. REC'D. IN SOCIAL FILES

White House Social Files, Alpha Files, "ORCHESTRA," Box 1589

Margaret Orcutt

Air Mail

Orcutt Desert Ranch,
Post Office Box 111,
Newberry Springs, California
92365
March 15, 1967

Dear President Johnson:

You are handling the Vietnam war situation with
courage. Because of which we can guess that your life and
the lives of your family have been threatened not once but
many times.

On the home front, in many instances the same can be
said. I am thinking of the new Interstate Highway System.

Projected Interstate 40 takes in over one-half mile
of my ranch and in this connection I would like to commend to
your attention a man who has worked under difficulties and
harassments; yet, he comes through with vision as well as understanding:

Mr Clyde V. Kane, District Engineer,
CALIFORNIA DIVISION OF HIGHWAYS,
District VIII,
San Bernardino, California 92403

For such men as you and me, we, the taxpayers, can
feel naught but respect and deep satisfaction.

Sincerely,

Miss Margaret Orcutt

President L. B. Johnson,
The White House,
Washington, D. C.

166

March 27, 1967

Dear Miss Orcutt:

President Johnson asked me to thank you
for your letter. It was good of you to
give him the benefit of your comments
and to assure him of your support.

With the President's best wishes,

Sincerely,

Paul M. Popple
Assistant to the President

Miss Margaret Orcutt
Orcutt Desert Ranch
Post Office Box 111
Newberry Springs, California 92365

MW:mss

About the Author

C. V. Wooster is an author, educator, and storyteller with a passion for exploring the lives of ordinary people who do extraordinary things. With a background in history and a keen interest in psychology, his writing brings depth and insight to stories of quiet defiance and personal conviction. He believes the most compelling narratives are often buried in forgotten headlines and unmarked roadsides.

In addition to *Mrs. Orcutt's Driveway*, Wooster is the author of *Imitation Nation*, a sharp cultural critique on authenticity in the modern world, and *History: Unattached*, a fresh and engaging dive into overlooked historical tales and the psychological motivations behind them. His work blends narrative, research, and reflection to honor those who shape the world in unexpected ways.

Wooster's writing has been praised for its emotional clarity, intellectual weight, and respectful attention to detail. He continues to seek out stories that deserve to be remembered.

To learn more, visit cvwooster.com.